En Suite

Joe O'Byrne

T0262426

Methuen

Methuen

1 3 5 7 9 10 8 6 4 2

Published in Great Britain in 2002 by
Methuen Publishing Limited
215 Vauxhall Bridge Road,
London SW1V 1EJ

Methuen Publishing Limited Reg. No. 3543167

A CIP catalogue record is available from the British Library

ISBN 0 413 77225 X

Typeset by SX Composing DTP, Rayleigh, Essex
Printed and bound in Great Britain by
Cox & Wyman Ltd, Reading, Berkshire

The National Theatre
The Abbey and Peacock Theatres

En Suite

By Joe O'Byrne

The National Theatre gratefully acknowledges the financial
support from the Arts Council/An Chomhairle Ealaíon

En Suite

By Joe O'Byrne

En Suite by Joe O'Byrne was first performed at the Peacock Theatre, Dublin on Thursday 14 March 2002. Press night was 20 March 2002.

The play is set in a small coastal town near Dublin

There will be one interval of 15 minutes

Cast

Evelyn	Marion O'Dwyer
Ella	Kelly Campbell
Emer	Lesley Conroy
Clara	Emma Colohan
Owen	Enda Oates
Hannes	Arthur Riordan
Lotte	Noelle Brown
Director	David Parnell
Designer	Ferdia Murphy
Lighting Designer	Tony Wakefield
Sound	Cormac Carroll
Stage Director	John Stapleton
Assistant Stage Manager	Catriona Behan
Voice Coach	Andrea Ainsworth
Set	Abbey Theatre Workshop
Costumes	Abbey Theatre Wardrobe Department

Please note that the text of the play which appears in this volume may be changed during the rehearsal process and appear in a slightly altered form in performance.

Joe O'Byrne *Author*

Joe's recent plays include **It Come Up Sun**, Passion Machine, 2000, **The Article**, Altes Schauspielhaus, Stuttgart, 2001 and **The Clearing Station**, Theatre of Joy, 2001. Last year he directed and adapted Oscar Wilde's **The Picture of Dorian Gray**, Irish Repertory Theatre, New York, translated Brecht's **Mother Courage and her Children**, Vesuvius Theatre Company and directed Patrick McCabe's **Loco County Lonesome**, Black Box Theatre Company. For many years he was Artistic Director of Co-Motion Theatre where he wrote and directed **Departed**, **The Ghost of Saint Joan** and **The Sinking of the Titanic and Other Matters**. He also directed Peter Weiss's **The Song of the White Man's Burden**, Georg Kaiser's **From Morning to Midnight**, the cabaret compilation **Cabaret/Kabarett**, Pat McCabe's **Frank Pig says Hello** and **The Drum** by Tony Kavanagh. At the Gate Theatre he directed **The Dumb Walter** for the first Pinter festival and for Macnas/Galway Arts Festival, Patrick McCabe's **The Dead School**. Film work includes the screenplay for the film **Korea** based on the John McGahern short story and his own first feature, **Pete's Meteor**.

David Parnell *Director*

David was born in Dublin and began his career with Dublin Youth Theatre, before training at the Samuel Beckett Centre, Trinity College. He has appeared as an actor throughout Ireland and abroad, including various roles at the Abbey and Peacock Theatres. David has been Staff Director at the National Theatre where his work has included assistant director on **Blackwater Angel**, national tour director on **A Life** and European tour director on **Translations**. He has also directed numerous play readings including **Royal Supreme** by Alex Johnston, **Due** by Tara Maria Lovett, **The Wrong Man** by Danny Morrison and **My Scandalous Life** by Thomas Kilroy. David's other directing work includes **The Taxi**, **Even the Trees** and **Teechers**, the Family Theatre Company, **Crowd-Scene**, DYT, **Sexual Perversity in Chicago**, AM Productions, **As You Like It** (co-director), Galway Youth Theatre, **Honesty**, Livestock Theatre Group, **The Ginger-Bread Mix-up**, Bickerstaffe Theatre Company, **Licking the Marmalade Spoon**, Project Arts Centre and **Shoot the Crow** for Druid Theatre Company. David is joint Artistic Director with Paul Meade of Gúna Nua Theatre Company where he directed **Four Stories** at project @ the mint, **Burn This**, Dublin Fringe Festival 2000 and **The Importance of Being Earnest** in co-production with the Civic Theatre, Tallaght. Most recently David and Paul co-wrote and directed **Scenes form a Water Cooler** which was awarded Best Production at Dublin Fringe 2001 and will undertake a national tour in April.

Ferdia Murphy *Designer*

Born in Dublin, Ferdia trained at Central Saint Martin's College of Art and Design in London, graduating in 1999. In Ireland, his designs include **A Quiet Life**, Peacock Theatre, **Blasted**, Bedrock Productions, **Richard III** and **Mutabilitie**, Theatreworks, **Playing from the Heart**, the Ark, **Dealer's Choice**, Lyric Theatre, **In the Dark Air of a Closed Room**, Loose Canon, **The Triumph of Love**, **The Dispute** and **Camino Royale** at the Samuel Beckett Centre and **Alternative Miss Ireland VI** and **VII** at the Olympia. In London he designed **Sweeney Todd** at the Bridewell Theatre, **The Consul** and **Inside Out** at the Cochrane Theatre and he co-designed **Bluebeard's Castle** at the Royal Festival Hall.

Tony Wakefield *Lighting Designer*

Tony Wakefield joined the National Theatre in 1964. He has designed lighting for both the Abbey and Peacock Theatres and his many credits include **The Great Hunger, The Playboy of the Western World** which toured extensively, **Too Late for Logic, The Gigli Concert, The Comedy of Errors, The Shadow of a Gunman,** which toured throughout Ireland, Australia and New Zealand, **Kitty O'Shea, Mamie Sighs, Prayers of Sherkin, Howling Moons Silent Sons, Away Alone, The Winter Thief, The Countess Cathleen, On the Outside/On the Inside, Hubert Murray's Widow, Brothers of the Brush, Asylum! Asylum!, Sheep's Milk on the Boil, Cré na Cille, A Picture of Paradise, Twenty Grand, As the Beast Sleeps, Sisters and Brothers, The Importance of Being Earnest, Kevin's Bed** and **A Life** which toured Ireland. Tony is Technical Director of the National Theatre.

Noelle Brown *Lotte*

Noelle trained at the Gaiety School of Acting in 1987. Her work at the Abbey and Peacock Theatres includes **Sarcophagus, Ghosts** which toured to New York and **Dancing at Lughnasa** which toured to Australia. Other theatre work includes **Bortstal Boy, Translations, The Scatterin,** Gaiety Theatre, **The Constant Couple, Happy Birthday Dear Alice,** Red Kettle, **Peer Gynt, Pride and Prejudice, A Christmas Carol,** Gate Theatre, **Hang all the Harpers,** Dubblejoint, **Fear of Feathers,** Wet Paint, **The Illusion,** Charabanc, **As You Like It, Hamlet, The Merchant of Venice, Macbeth,** Second Age Theatre, **The Whisperers,** Rough Magic, Edinburgh Festival, **The Plains of Enna,** Tivoli Theatre, **The Starchild and Other Stories, Ladies and Gentlemen,** Project Arts Centre, **Learning to Love Doreen Nolan,** Druid Theatre and **Zoe's Play,** The Ark and Kennedy Center, Washington. Television includes **Molloy, Private Lives, Fair City, Upwardly Mobile, Father Ted, The Governor, The Ambassador, Making the Cut, Glenroe, Bachelors Walk, No Tears** and the films **Bogwoman** and **Day One.** She recently directed **The Belle of Amherst** by William Luce at Bewleys Theatre Café.

Kelly Campbell *Ella*

Kelly trained at the University of Ulster, the Central School of Speech and Drama and with the SITI Company, New York. She last appeared at the Abbey and Peacock Theatres in **Iphigenia at Aulis** and **Tartuffe.** Other theatre work includes **In Camera, Medea** and **The Crucible,** Riverside Theatre Coleraine, **You have been Watching,** Primitive Science, South Bank, London, **Lasst des Golders,** Bern and Zurich International Theatre Festival. She is a Director of Bewley's Café Theatre where she directed **How she Lied to her Husband** and **The Wit of a Sparrow** and performed in **Lovely Betty.** Film and television work includes **Mystic Knights, Black Day at Black Rock, Buy Me, Geraldo, Everything's under Control** and **The Magnificent Ambersons.**

Emma Colohan *Clara*

Emma graduated form the Actor Training Course at Trinity College in 2000. While there she performed in **Tis Pity She's a Whore,** directed by Jason Byrne, **Attempts on her Life,** directed by Brian Brady and **Artists and**

Admirers directed by Lily-Susan Todd. Since graduating she played in **Iphigenia at Aulis**, Abbey Theatre, **The Countrywoman**, Upstate Theatre Project, **The Grapes of Wrath** with Storytellers Theatre Company and **Midden** with Rough Magic at the Hampstead Theatre, London.

Leslie Conroy *Emer*

Lesley is originally from Cork. She trained at the Samuel Beckett Centre, Trinity College. In 2000 she trained extensively with Loose Canon Theatre Company, exploring the nature of physical theatre. Previous productions at the Abbey and Peacock Theatres include **Something's in the Way, Cúirt an Mheán Oíche** and **Caoineadh Airt Uí Laoghaire**. Recent theatre work includes **Another 24 Hours, Epiphany**, Semper Fi, **Alphabet** which launched the 2001 Dublin Fringe Festival, **In the Dark Air of A Closed Room, The Duchess of Malfi** and **The Spanish Tragedy**, Loose Canon, **A Clockwork Orange** and **Animal Farm**, Corcadorca, **Medea Material**, Bedrock Productions, **An Triail** and **Milseog an tSamhraidh**, Amharclann de hÍde. Films include **A Man of Few Words, Saltwater, Short, Brothers in Arms** and **Angela Mooney Dies Again**. Television credits include **Ri Ra** and **Kaisleán Klaus**. She played the title role in **Sive** for *Festival 75: A Feast of Drama* for RTE Radio 1.

Enda Oates *Owen*

Enda has worked in most Irish theatres for the last twelve years. Work at the Abbey and Peacock Theatres include **Saint Joan, The Corsican Brothers, Big Maggie, A Child's Christmas in Wales, Madigans Lock, The Devil's Disciple, Colours, A Happy Journey** and **Blinded by the Light**. Work at the Gate Theatre includes **Jacques Brel is Alive and Well** and **Juno and the Paycock** (including tour to Jerusalem and Broadway). He has also worked with Rough Magic, Field Day and the Passion Machine theatre companies. Recent work includes **The Chastitute, Matchmake Me Do**, Tivoli Theatre, **Gulliver's Travels**, Galloglass Theatre Company, **True Believers, The Plains of Enna**, Fishamble Theatre Company, **Uncle Vanya**, Tricycle Theatre, London and Irish tour, **Buddleia, Studs**, Passion Machine (Project Arts Centre and Donmar Warehouse), **The Plough and the Stars**, Young Vic and **The Field**, Gaiety Theatre. He acted in and was an associate producer of Edward Farrell's touring production of **The Country Boy**. Television and film work includes **Ballykissangel, Glenroe, Upwardly Mobile, The Ambassador, Ordinary Decent Criminal, A Man of No Importance, All for Love, Cycle of Violence, Crossmaheart, The Governor, Fools of Fortune, Remington Steele, Errors and Omissions, Small World** and **Henry V**.

Marion O'Dwyer *Evelyn*

Marion's previous appearances at the Abbey and Peacock Theatres include **The Memory of Water, Kevin's Bed, The Only True History of Lizzie Finn, Portia Coughlan** at the Peacock and the Royal Court, London, **Moving, You Can't Take it with You, The Silver Tassie** and **Dancing at Lughnasa** which also toured Ireland and Australia and **Wonderful Tennessee** in which she also played on Broadway. Appearances at the Gate Theatre include Stella in

Stella by Starlight, A Tale of Two Cities, Pride and Prejudice, The Threepenny Opera, Fathers and Sons, Blithe Spirit, Twelfth Night and An Ideal Husband. For Druid Theatre Company she played in The Donahue Sisters, Lovers' Meeting, Poor Beast in the Rain and The Loves of Cass Maguire. Other theatre work includes Molly in Molly Sweeney for the Bristol Old Vic, Mena in Sive at the Watford Palace Theatre and Tricycle Theatre, London, Liz in From Both Hips for Fishamble Theatre Company at project @ the mint and the Tron Theatre, Glasgow. Marion co-starred in Anjelica Houston's film Agnes Browne. Other film and television work includes Oonagh in Ballykissangel, appearances in The Ambassador, Rebel Heart, The Life of Reilly, Finbarr's Class and Thou shalt not Kill. Marion was a member of the RTE Players on radio. Marion's radio work includes the recent BBC Radio 4 series Faithful Departed and she was a member of the RTE Players for four years. She also directed Long Lonely Time at Andrews Lane Theatre.

Arthur Riordan *Hannes*

Arthur's previous work at the Abbey and Peacock Theatres includes The Comedy of Errors and The Last Apache Reunion. He is a founder member of Rough Magic and has appeared in many of their productions including Digging for Fire and most recently, The Whisperers. Other work includes The Lonesome West, St. Patrick's Day, Druid Theatre, Massive Damages, Studs, Passion Machine, Happy Birthday Dear Alice, Red Kettle, The Gay Detective, Troubled Hearts, Project Arts Centre, Wired to the Moon, Fishamble, The Star Child, Storytellers and Rap Fire with Bickerstaffe which Arthur co-wrote with Des Bishop. Arthur's other written work includes Hidden Charges, MC Dev's Emergency Session, both for Rough Magic, Love Me?!, Corn Exchange Car Show and The Last Temptation of Michael Flatley, Macra na Feirme. Film and television work includes Borstal Boy, Black Day at Black Rock, My Dinner with Oswald, Rat, On the Edge, Joyce and Beckett Play Pitch and Putt, The Last September, Angela Mooney Dies Again, The Ambassador and No Tears.

Amharclann Na Mainistreach
The National Theatre

PERSONNEL

Artistic Director
Ben Barnes

Managing Director
Richard Wakely

General Manager
Martin Fahy

Director's Office
Ciara Flynn
(P.A. Artistic Director)
Grainne Howe
(P.A. Managing Director)

Peacock Director
Ali Curran

Associate Directors
Garry Hynes
Laszlo Marton
Paul Mercier
Katie Mitchell
Conall Morrison
Lynne Parker
Deborah Warner

Honorary Associate Directors
Vincent Dowling
Tomas MacAnna

Abbey Players
Clive Geraghty
Des Cave

Staff Director
David Parnell

Casting Director
Marie Kelly

Voice Coach
Andrea Ainsworth

Writer-in-Association
sponsored by
Anglo Irish Bank
Jim Nolan

Archive
Mairead Delaney
(Archivist)

Box Office
Adam Lawlor
(Box Office Manager)

Des Byrne
(Box Office Assistant)
Clare Downey
(Chief Cashier)

Box Office Clerks
Catherine Casey
Anne Marie Doyle
Edel Hanly
Lorraine Hanna
Maureen Robertson
David Windrim

Front of House
Pauline Morrison
(House Manager)
John Baynes
(Deputy House Manager)

Cleaning
Joe McNamara
(Supervisor)

Reception
Niamh Douglas
(Senior Receptionist)
Sandra Williams
(Receptionist)

Stage Door
Patrick Gannon
Patrick Whelan

Ushers
Jim O'Keeffe (Chief Usher)
Daniel Byrne
Ruth Colgan
Con Doyle
Ivan Kavanagh
Simon Lawlor
Seamus Mallin
Fred Murray

Education
Sharon Murphy
(Head of Outreach/Education)
Sarah Jordan
(Administrator)
Jean O'Dwyer
(Projects Officer)
Joanna Parkes
(Projects Officer)

Finance
Margaret Bradley
(Financial Controller)
Margaret Flynn
(Accounts)
Pat O'Connell (Payroll)

Literary
Jocelyn Clarke
(Commissioning Mgr.)
Orla Flanagan
(Literary Officer)
Karin McCully
(Senior Reader)

Press and Marketing
Press Representation
Kate Bowe PR
Katherine Brownridge
(Marketing Manager)
Tina Connell
(Promotions Officer)
Lucy McKeever (Press & Programmes Officer)

Technical
Tony Wakefield
(Technical Director)
Tommy Nolan
(Production Manager)
Peter Rose
(Construction Manager)
Vanessa Fitz-Simon
(Asst. Production Manager)

Carpenters
Mark Joseph Darley
(Master Carpenter)
John Kavanagh (Deputy)
Brian Comiskey
Bart O'Farrell
Kenneth Crowe
(Assistant)

Scenic Artists
Angie Benner
Jennifer Moonan

Design
Emma Cullen
(Design Assistant)

Electricians
Mick Doyle
(Chief Electrician)
Brian Fairbrother

Joe Glasgow
Barry Madden
Kevin McFadden
(Acting Deputy)

Information Technology
Dave O'Brien (Manager)

Maintenance
Brian Fennell
(Maintenance Engineer)
Tony Delaney (Assistant)

Props
Stephen Molloy
(Property Master)

Stage Managers
John Andrews
Gerry Doyle

Stage Hands
Aaron Clear
Mick Doyle (Fly Master)
Pat Dillon (Deputy Stage Managers)
Paul Kelly

Stage Directors
Finola Eustace
(Head of Department)
John Stapleton
Audrey Hession

Assistant Stage Managers
Stephen Dempsey
Maree Kearns

Sound
Dave Nolan
(Chief Sound Technician)
Cormac Carroll
Nuala Golden

Wardrobe
Joan O'Clery (Acting Wardrobe Supervisor)
Fiona Talbot (Acting Deputy)
Angela Hanna
Vicky Miller
Catherine Fay
Frances Kelly
(Wigs & Hairdressing)
Patsy Giles (Make-Up)

Amharclann Na Mainistreach
The National Theatre

En Suite

Characters

Evelyn Dwyer, a woman in her late thirties.
Ella, her daughter, early twenties.
Emer, her daughter, nineteen.
Owen Mahon, Evelyn's brother, early forties.
Clara Thomson, a friend of Ella's, mid-twenties.
Hannes, a big German man in his forties.
Lotte, a German woman in her forties.

Set

Acts One, Two, Three, Five take place in the kitchen of
Evelyn Dwyer's bed and breakfast. Act Four takes place on
a cliff.

The kitchen should have a door to stage right which leads
to the guests' dining room, a door at the back to the hall,
and one at stage left that leads outside.

During Act Five the set is disassembled. How this is done
will vary from design to design.

Prelude

The kitchen of a modern-looking bed and breakfast. Above the kitchen, a seascape with a lighthouse; to one side the suggestion of cliffs.

Music.

At first we hear **Clara**'s *voice, and only vaguely see her deep in the stage.*

Clara   If you look along the coast, ladies and gentlemen, you'll see the Martello Tower built during the Napoleonic era by the British as a system of watchtowers in case of French invasion. You'll find them studded all along the coast, and the one in Sandycove has become famous as the location of the opening chapter of James Joyce's *Ulysses*. Further down the coast you'll see the footbridge over the railway line, which is known as the 'Lady's Stairs' because of a certain lady in white who is reputedly seen to walk there at night.

By now **Clara** *has appeared around the set, and faces the audience.*

And out there the lighthouse, where once my father worked, which, on a foggy night, will turn this small coastal area into a magical land with its sweeping light. And you'll see many other places of less interest, many houses with a story, because every house has a story, and sometimes it's hard to imagine how a single roof can contain them all . . .

She turns and looks into the set. The sounds of the house: showers, toilets flushing, doors opening and closing, etc. The sounds change to those of cutlery, a kettle boiling, etc. The music fades out.

Act One

Evelyn *comes rushing in from the guests' dining-room, still watched by* **Clara** *from downstage.*

Evelyn They want pancakes! Why can't they be like everyone else and eat an ordinary breakfast that'll give them a heart attack sooner rather than later.

She takes flour from a press and pours it into a bowl, then beats in eggs and pours in milk and starts beating the mix. **Clara** *moves away, towards stage left, and exits.*

Evelyn Bed and Burden! Bed and Bedlam! Bed and Bedamned! Bed and Bastard!

A young woman, **Ella Dwyer**, *comes in from the hall and sits down at the table. She pours a cup of tea and sips it. In the background,* **Evelyn** *is cooking, and she continues to mutter to herself: 'Bed and Bejaysus! Bed and Bollax!' etc. She has the pancakes ready and she rushes out with them. She comes back in and sees* **Ella**.

Evelyn You up at last? My God, they've been driving me crazy all morning. One of them sent back the fry, wanted it cooked in olive oil! A fry-up cooked in olive oil, what's the world coming to! And the pancakes! I must take them off the menu! Are you listening to me?

Ella *doesn't respond.* **Evelyn** *comes right up to her.*

Evelyn Are you listening to me? Don't you listen to your mother any more?

Ella *puts the headset of her Walkman on and listens to music.*

Evelyn That's it, lock yourself in, and let your mother do all the work! What'll you do if I hang myself? What'll you do then? Then you'll have to get your own breakfast, won't you? Now, where'll I hang myself? I'll do it over the kitchen table, the very place! Or maybe I'll drown myself! That'd be better. Down by the point! But no, hanging over the kitchen table would be better.

She comes up behind **Ella** *and does a little dance to the techno beat that can be heard from the Walkman, and then pulls the headset off* **Ella** *and shouts into her ear:*

Bed and Burden! Bed and Bedlam! Bed and Bugger! Bed and Bastard! Bed and Bollax! Bed and Bumfuck!

As she says these things, **Ella** *starts to sing the 'Ave Maria'. The louder* **Evelyn** *gets, the louder* **Ella** *sings.* **Lotte**, *a German woman, appears at the dining-room door.*

Lotte   Hello! Hello! Hello! (*Shouts.*) Hello!

Evelyn *looks around.*

Lotte (*in German accent*)   If we can have some more brown bread. I asked you two times soon.

Evelyn *rushes to the bread bin and slices thick wedges of brown bread.*

Evelyn   We like to sing hymns at breakfast, it's a great way to start the day!

She hands a heap of brown bread to **Lotte** *on a plate.*

There you are now, all the brown bread you can eat.

Lotte *goes back into the dining-room.*

Evelyn   That one's been driving me mad all morning with her olive oil and if they eat any more brown bread they'll end up blocking up that toilet and the sewers as well probably, and then I'll have a lovely job to do! Oh yes, that'll just make my day!

Ella *stops singing.*

Evelyn   What'll the guests think if you go singing hymns like that!

Ella *puts the headphones back on.*

Evelyn   Where did I go wrong? (*Looks around.*) No bluebottles, that's one small mercy this morning!

She goes to the dining-room door, puts on a smile and goes out. **Ella** *looks around and takes off her headphones. She picks up the phone and dials.*

Ella   Hi, it's me. Yeh, I slept all right, but I was a bit lonely. And you? (*Listens.*)

Evelyn *comes back in carrying dishes, still holding the smile, which she drops as soon as she enters the kitchen. She puts the dishes down and watches* **Ella**.

Ella   OK, I'll call over in a little while. Kisses.

Evelyn *comes up to her as she puts the phone down.*

Evelyn   Who was that?

Ella   None of your business.

Evelyn   I'm paying for that call.

Ella *takes money out of her pocket and slams it on the table.*

Ella   Ten, fifteen, seventeen, nineteen, twenty – twenty cents, take it!

Evelyn   I can get the phone company to itemise the bill, and I'll find out, all I have to do is remember the time and date of the call.

Ella   Do that!

Evelyn *takes the money.*

Evelyn   Will you take breakfast up to your sister?

Ella   She can come down and get it herself.

Evelyn   OK, I'll do it myself.

Ella   Mum, she's pregnant, she's not an invalid.

Evelyn   Bed and Bastard!

Ella   Mum, will you stop that!

Evelyn   Stop what?

Ella   That gibberish.

Evelyn   It helps me get through the day. Bed and Bastard!

Ella   Mum!

Evelyn   You and your sister, you've driven me to it!

Ella   If you're so unhappy, Mum, burn the place down!

Evelyn   And then I'll hang myself from the tree outside.

Ella   That's a good idea.

Evelyn   Such a thoughtful daughter.

Ella   Mum, you make it sound as if you're in prison here.

Evelyn   A life sentence. Bed and Bedead. Your father knew what he was doing, oh, he did! One of his cronies must've told him, if your wife is going to have a nervous breakdown, buy a B&B, that'll give her something to do, something to occupy her time with. And then bugger off and leave her and you won't have a guilty conscience because she has a way of making ends meet.

Ella   Mum, you need to find God.

Evelyn   Is he lost?

Ella   Very funny, Mum!

Evelyn   What did I do to deserve you?

Ella   You know right well what you did.

Evelyn   Oh, I do, do I? (*Getting shriller.*) Do I? Do I? Do I? Oh, it's too early in the day to be having an argument like this.

She looks around, then picks up a swatter and tries to hit the bluebottle.

I'm just sick of bluebottles! (*She swats.*) Got you!

Ella   Long live the bluebottle!

Evelyn   Not in this kitchen! I don't want government health inspectors down on me!

Ella   As if they'd bother with you!

Evelyn   Have you nothing to do?

Ella   Guessed right!

Evelyn   Well I'm just going to wash all these dishes, set the dining-room, make all the beds, clean out all the rooms, scrub the floors, wash the dirty towels, sheets . . .   .

Ella   Mum, you can easily afford to pay someone to do that for you. You're just too mean.

Evelyn   Mean! How do you like that, mean!

Ella *leaves the kitchen.*

Evelyn   Mean! The cheek of that!

She goes to the sink.

Bed and Barearsed! Mean! What would she know about mean! What does she know about the cost of sausages and rashers and eggs and cornflakes and bread and butter and black and white pudding and milk and olive oil! And if those two hussies were any good, I wouldn't need anyone else, they should be doing it all for nothing to help me out, isn't that what daughters are for? Olive oil! A fry-up cooked in olive oil, that's the best yet! What's wrong with good old-fashioned lard? And mean, she says! And that singing! Ave Maria! Ave Maria, my arse!

She slams the dishes down.

Oh yes. (*Sings.*) Ave fuckin' Maria!

She shakes her head and then goes back to doing the dishes. The door opens and **Emer** *comes into the kitchen with difficulty as she is quite pregnant. She sits down.*

Emer   Anything for breakfast, Mum?

Evelyn (*to herself*)   Bed and Bastard!

Emer   Mum!

Evelyn (*sweetly*)   Yes, love!

Emer   What's for breakfast?

Evelyn   Anything you like, honey.

Emer   I'd love pancakes.

Evelyn (*to herself*)   Pancakes!

Evelyn *continues to do the dishes noisily.*

Emer   Mum!

Evelyn   Yes, love.

Emer   Didn't you hear me?

Evelyn   You could make them yourself.

Emer   But you make them so well, Mum.

Evelyn   I do, don't I?

Emer   Ah, Mum!

Evelyn   There's cornflakes there. And I've some sausages and toast left over.

Emer   Leftovers again!

Evelyn   Waste not, want not.

Emer   That's disgusting, Mum, eating the guests' leftovers.

Evelyn   You're one to be talking and you a guest's leftover.

Emer (*angry*)   Mum!

Evelyn   Well, it's true, isn't it? Isn't it! I should advertise . . . 'The best of breakfast and the most comfortable of rooms, all en suite, and if you feel like a little extra, well, you can always try one of the daughters of the proprietress, no extra charge.'

Emer   Mum!

Evelyn   What was his name. I keep forgetting it.

Emer   No, you don't.

Evelyn   Don Giovanni.

Emer   Gianni, short for Giovanni.

Evelyn   He was short, all right. Yeh, he was a stocky little runt . . .

Emer   Mum! Drop it!

Evelyn   Bed and Bastard!

Emer   Mum!

Evelyn   Yes, love?

Emer   I'll have those leftover sausages then.

Evelyn *gets them and places them in front of her.*

Evelyn   There you are, love.

Emer *eats as* **Evelyn** *goes back to washing the dishes.* **Emer** *stops.*

Evelyn (*under her breath*)   A dirty little bug-eyed Eyetalian bastard of a bed hopper! Bed and Brasser!

Emer   Mum, he kicked again.

Evelyn (*to herself*)   He didn't kick hard enough, if you ask me! (*Loudly to* **Emer**.) Did he?

Emer (*feeling her stomach*)   Do you want to feel him, Mum.

Hesitantly, **Evelyn** *comes over and puts her hand on* **Emer***'s stomach. She holds her hand there for a few moments, then goes back to the kitchen sink, and plunges her hands back into the sink.*

Evelyn   Who's your sister seeing?

Emer   I don't know, Mum.

Evelyn   You do.

Emer   I don't.

The doorbell rings.

Evelyn   Is it the young McCormack fella?

Emer   There's someone at the door, Mum.

Evelyn   I know she's older than you, but I worry about her more. This religious stuff . . . what's that all about?

Emer   Beats me.

Evelyn   Beats me? What kind of talk is that? It's not good Irish talk anyway. Don't you know what your sister is up to? Don't you two ever talk?

Emer   No.

Evelyn   No?

Emer   You know we don't, Mum.

Evelyn   Ye're two eggs out of the same basket, I don't see why you don't get on.

Emer   She's just jealous of me, that's all, Mum.

Evelyn   Jealous of you?

Emer   Yeh, jealous of me. She always was. Because I was your favourite.

Evelyn   No, you weren't. I never had favourites, I always treated you two like cups from the same set . . .

Emer   She always gave me a hard time because of it.

Evelyn   Oh, everything is always my fault, isn't it? I can't ever do anything right! I try to bring you two up . . . in a modern way, and what happens? One turns into a nun, the other into a whore. Beats me! Yeh, it beats me all right!

She washes the dishes at a furious and angry pace. The doorbell rings again.

Emer   Mum, there's someone at the door.

Evelyn   Can't you go.

Emer   Mum!

Emer *gets up and goes out.*

Evelyn   I hope they're not British . . . or French . . . or German . . . or anything! I'm sick of the way they come parading in here, they think now we're all in the EU together they can just come right in here and take over. The cheek of one of them German fellas, telling me they were paying our bills, giving us EC handouts to keep our country afloat. And that Belgian couple, my grandfather fought in World War One for that little country, and the gratitude they showed, complaints about this, that and the other, and it was the final straw when they got up on their high horses about the shower, it only dribbles, he said . . . it only dribbles he says! Had to give him a fiver off for it. That's the gratitude you get. Granda would've gone mad if he was alive to hear that. The gratitude! It beats me! It all beats me! I surrender, I'm beaten. Put me in front of the firing squad! Take aim! Fire!

Emer *comes back in, leading in* **Owen**, *who is slightly older than* **Evelyn**.

Owen   Hello!

Evelyn   Beats me!

Owen (*louder*)   Hello!

Evelyn *turns around, and when she does she jumps, sending dishes flying into the air.* **Emer** *sits down at the table again.*

Owen   Evelyn.

Evelyn (*barely able to speak*)   Owen . . . Owen . . . what . . . ?

Owen *goes to her and they embrace.*

Evelyn   Emer . . . Emer . . . this is your Uncle Owen.

Owen *turns to her and they shake hands.*

Owen   Even more beautiful than in the photographs.

Evelyn   But what are you . . . you never wrote . . .

Owen   A sudden impulse.

Evelyn   But why?

There is a silence.

Owen   Why?

Evelyn   Why?

Owen   Why?

Evelyn.   Why?

Owen   Why?

Evelyn   Why?

Owen   Why?

Evelyn   Stop saying why!

She stops, realising somehow she has confused herself. Another silence.

Emer   So, what's Las Vegas like, Uncle Owen? You were in Las Vegas, weren't you?

Evelyn   Have you nothing to be doing? Shouldn't you be getting some exercise?

Emer   No.

Evelyn *gives her the daggers.*

Emer   OK, Mum. But I want to hear all about Las Vegas later, Uncle Owen.

She gets up and leaves the kitchen.

Evelyn   What are you doing home, Owen?

Owen   She's the younger, isn't she? Where's . . . ?

Evelyn   Ella? She's upstairs saying her prayers.

Owen   Prayers?

Evelyn   She's found religion.

Owen *looks serious, then he bursts out laughing.*

Owen   Religion!

Evelyn   It's not funny, Owen.

Owen *laughs again.*

Evelyn   What are you doing home, Owen?

Owen   Religion! That's a turn-up for the books.

Evelyn   What are you doing home, Owen?

Owen   That's the best yet.

Evelyn *(firmly)*   What are you doing home, Owen?

He bursts out laughing again, a little more uncontrollably. As he recovers, silence.

Evelyn   Owen, what are you doing home?

Owen   I'm sick, Evelyn. I came home to die.

Evelyn *looks at him in stunned silence. Then she bursts out crying.*

Evelyn   Oh, Owen, what's wrong with you?

Owen   Inoperable brain tumour. About six months. They advised me not to travel, but I didn't want to die over there.

Evelyn   Oh, no, Owen, oh no, oh my God, oh no!

Owen   Evelyn, I'm ready for it.

Evelyn   But you're only forty-two.

Owen   If my time has come, my time has come.

The door opens and **Ella** *appears in the kitchen.* **Evelyn** *starts to wipe her tears.*

Owen   And this must be Ella.

He stands up.

Evelyn   This is your Uncle Owen, love.

Ella   Why are you crying, Mum?

Evelyn   I'm just so happy to see him.

Owen   She's the image of you, Evelyn.

Evelyn   She is, isn't she?

Owen   Your mother says you found religion.

Ella   And you found gambling.

Owen   Oh, I wouldn't say that.

Ella   You lost everything?

Evelyn   Ella! Don't say things like that!

Ella   Well, he's never been home before.

Evelyn   Ella, he's . . .

Owen   Evelyn, don't.

Evelyn   Ella, he's . . . going to die.

Evelyn *bursts out crying again.* **Ella** *looks at* **Owen** *closely.*

Ella   Are you?

Owen *doesn't answer. He puts his arm around* **Evelyn**.

Owen   It's all right, Evelyn.

Ella   Are you?

Owen   Yes.

Ella   God can be cruel.

Owen   He can.

Ella   And merciful.

Owen   Not your fault.

Ella   Why would it be my fault?

Owen   Oh, nothing, no, nothing. My fault.

Ella   Your fault?

Silence.

Ella   You know, Uncle Owen, Mum always worried about you.

Evelyn   Ella, he doesn't need to hear about that.

Ella   Yes, he does.

Owen   I know she did.

Ella   Every Christmas she'd say, next Christmas he'll be home.

Evelyn   Ella, can't you be nice to your uncle.

Ella   He doesn't mind.

Owen   I don't.

Ella   Now he knows.

Evelyn *sees something and grabs the swat.*

Evelyn   A bluebottle, Owen, they're the bane of my life!

She swats at it vigorously. **Ella** *throws her eyes to heaven.*

Ella   Anyway, got to go, someone to see.

Ella *looks at* **Owen**, *then rushes out of the room.* **Evelyn** *manages to swat the bluebottle.*

Evelyn   That's two today so far!

Owen   Murder.

Evelyn   What? Don't be saying things like that. It was only a bluebottle.

Owen *looks to the door where* **Ella** *left.*

Owen   She is . . . beautiful.

Evelyn   She is . . .

Owen   She looks like you . . . that's good . . . that's good . . . good that she takes her looks from you. But the religion . . .

He laughs.

Evelyn   Don't laugh.

The doorbell rings. She stands up.

Evelyn   That damned doorbell!

She rushes out. **Owen** *looks around at the kitchen, puts his hands to his head, as if in pain, then gets to his knees.* **Evelyn** *comes rushing back in with a package, picks up her purse.*

The butcher.

She runs out again. **Owen** *places his head on the ground.* **Evelyn** *comes back in.*

Owen. Owen! What are you doing? Oh God, Owen, you aren't dying now, are you? Owen! Owen!

He raises his head.

Evelyn   Oh, Owen, don't do that, you'll give me a heart attack. (*Pause.*) What are you doing? Get up! Get up, before someone comes in. Owen, get up!

Owen   The last few years haven't been good to me, Evelyn. I'm beat.

Evelyn   You too. You and me like two eggs into the pancake batter. Pancakes, did you ever hear the like in an Irish B&B for breakfast! (*She looks at him.*) Ella was right, wasn't she? You've lost everything?

Owen   I've lost.

Evelyn   Everything?

Owen   It'd been coming . . . a long time. Everything, like water through my fingers . . .

Silence.

Evelyn   Have you nothing left? No money?

Owen *shakes his head.* **Evelyn** *rushes to her purse.*

Owen (*quietly*)   Someone had it in for me . . .

Evelyn takes some notes out and gives them to him. **Owen** *looks at the notes, then puts them in his pocket.*

Owen　My sister. Just look at you . . .

Evelyn　Owen . . .

Owen　Just look at you . . .

Evelyn　Owen . . .

Owen　Just look at you . . .

Evelyn　Owen . . . don't keep saying that, you're like a scratched record.

The doorbell rings.

Owen　Just look at you . . .

Evelyn　Are you going to stay like that?

Owen　Just look at you . . .

Evelyn　Owen! Owen! Get up! Get up! And stop saying 'just look at you'!

The doorbell rings again.

(*To herself.*) Thank God for that doorbell.

She rushes out. She comes rushing back in. She grabs a key off a rail and rushes back out again.

Owen (*quietly*)　Nothing! Nothing! Nothing!

Evelyn *comes rushing back in, stops, catches her breath, and looks around.*

Evelyn　You'll stay here?

Owen　I don't have anywhere else.

Evelyn　No, 'course not.

Owen　I'll be just like another guest.

Evelyn　Guests pay.

Owen   Are you going to charge me?

Evelyn   No, no, no! I was only saying. (*Pause.*) That your only case?

Owen *nods.*

Evelyn   That's a life.

Silence.

I'll show you to your room.

Evelyn *picks up the case.* **Owen** *gets up off his knees.* **Evelyn** *leaves the kitchen.* **Owen** *follows her.*

Act Two

*It is night. A door opens and we hear **Ella** and **Clara** giggling. Faintly, in the background, a foghorn.*

Ella   Ssssh, the whole of Europe could wake up.

Clara   Meine Damen und Herren, Mesdames et Messieurs, Ladies and Gentlemen, I give you Ella Dwyer, the sexiest, raunchiest little tart you've ever clapped eyes on . . .

*Ella puts her hand over **Clara**'s mouth and she continues with further words, but muffled.*

Ella   Stop, Clara, stop!

Clara   *Merde! Puta! Bumsen! Coño! Achtung! Per favore!*

They laugh again.

Ella   Someone'll come in.

Clara   Who?

Ella   I don't know. Guests.

Clara   Ghosts?

Ella   No, guests. You've got ghosts on the brain. I bet when you're giving the guided tours to the tourists, you make up wild stories about ghosts and murders and werewolves to keep them happy?

Clara   I spice it up, yeh, of course.

*Clara leans in to kiss her. **Ella** backs away and blesses herself. As she is doing this, **Clara** grabs her hand to stop her. They struggle and **Ella** gets her hand free and slaps **Clara** on the face.*

Ella   Oh, I'm sorry.

*She proceeds to kiss **Clara** all over the face, repeating her apologies.*

Clara   You know, all this religious stuff is a real turn-off.

Ella   'Hail Mary, full of Grace . . .'

Clara *puts her hand over* **Ella***'s mouth.* **Ella** *pulls it away.*
Clara *leans in to kiss her when someone comes into the kitchen. It is*
Owen. **Clara** *and* **Ella** *jump.* **Owen** *sits at the table and takes a
deck of cards out of his pocket and then shuffles them.*

Clara (*quietly*)   Who's that?

Ella   My Uncle Owen.

Clara   You never said he was coming home.

Ella   Surprised us all, out of the blue.

Owen *stops and looks at them, then back at the cards, which he
places on the table.*

Owen   Nothing! Nothing! Nothing!

*He puts his hands to his head and holds it, then he gets up and starts
walking around the kitchen.* **Clara** *and* **Ella** *have to evade him.
Suddenly he starts shouting.*

Left me nothing, you've left me nothing! Nothing! Nothing!
Nothing!

Ella *and* **Clara** *are scared.* **Owen** *continues shouting 'Nothing!
Nothing!'* **Evelyn** *comes rushing into the kitchen and switches on the
light.*

Evelyn   What's going on? What's going on?

Ella   He just came in and started shouting.

Evelyn *goes to him and tries to calm him down, but he struggles with
her.*

Owen   Who are you? Go away! Go away! Who are you?

Evelyn   Owen, it's your sister. Evelyn. It's Evelyn.

Lotte *comes in the door.*

Lotte   Hello. There is much noise down here?

Evelyn *goes to her and tries to block her view.* **Owen** *goes wild, and stretches out his hands as if to someone's neck, and then he seems to wrestle and struggle with somebody invisible.*

Owen   I have to do it! I have to! You have to die! To die! Die! Die! Die!

Lotte   What is the matter with the man?

Evelyn   Oh, it's just a little old Irish custom.

Lotte   It looks to me as if he is possessed.

Evelyn   No, no, just a drop too much whiskey.

Owen *falls around the kitchen, but his cries, which still are 'Die! Die!', have become weaker, until he ends up on the ground in a ball, apparently weeping.*

Evelyn   Now, it's all over.

Lotte   I think he needs help.

Evelyn (*losing it*)   Go back up to your room or I'll charge you extra for the show.

Lotte   Maybe he needs the special priest, the exorcist.

Evelyn   You've been watching too many films, lady! He's just a sick man! He's going to die, so now if you don't mind, could we just get on with it on our own.

Lotte   I hope he does not die tonight.

She leaves the kitchen. **Evelyn** *approaches* **Owen** *cautiously.*

Evelyn   Owen, Owen, sit down here.

She leads him back to the chair at the table.

Clara   Who's going to die?

He doesn't answer. **Evelyn** *looks at* **Clara**.

Evelyn   And you're . . . ?

Clara   Clara Thomson.

Evelyn   Oh, yes, yes, you're the one that's started doing the guided tours. I have your flyers in the hall. Your mother is a teacher, isn't she? She used to teach you, didn't she, Ella? And your father? I don't know your father. What does he do?

Clara   He used to be a lighthouse man.

Ella   Till they computerised him out of a job.

Evelyn   Oh, yeh, of course, I've seen him about, on the cliffs.

Clara   Yeh, that's where you used to find him, but he died.

Evelyn   Oh yes, he did, didn't he? I'm sorry. When was that?

Clara   Over two years ago.

Evelyn   Oh yes, I remember now. A heart attack, wasn't it? Up on the cliffs. This place has the memory eaten up on me, with all I have to remember. I'm sorry for your trouble.

Ella   Mum, it was over two years ago!

Evelyn   Yes, yes, I know, but you never forget someone dying. I'm lucky my parents are still alive. We don't see them much, they moved to Sligo when Dad retired.

Ella   They're boring.

Evelyn   They're not! And Owen, you'll be going up to see them, won't you? They'll be glad you're home.

Owen *sits up a little.*

Evelyn   Owen, Owen . . .

Owen   Is that you, Evelyn?

Evelyn   Of course it is.

Owen   Where am I?

Evelyn   You're in 'The Bower, Bed and Breakfast'.

Owen (*weakly*)   Of course . . . of course . . .

Slowly she helps him up off the ground and leads him to the table.

Owen   I hope I didn't wake up the whole house.

Evelyn   Just Germany.

Ella *and* **Clara** *look at each other. Silence.*

Evelyn   We better get you back to bed, Owen.

She takes him by the elbow.

Come on, Owen, I'll take you up to your room.

Owen   The rooms are nice, and en suite! A bathroom in every room! It's all en suite, not like the old days.

Evelyn   Won't get the guests any other way these days.

Owen   En suite . . . not like the old days . . .

He stands up, but he goes up to **Ella**, *takes her by the head and stares at her.*

Owen   She's very beautiful, isn't she? (*Looking into her eyes.*) Yes, those eyes.

He turns and walks out of the kitchen with **Evelyn**. *Silence.*

Clara   So, when was the last time he was home?

Ella   Twenty years ago, I think, more maybe. As far as I know he left before I was born, hasn't been back since. He must've hated the place. Don't blame him. I can't wait to get out.

Clara   He must've done something bad then.

Ella   We could leave together.

Clara   But don't you think it's strange he never came back to see his parents, or your mother?

Ella   Oh, let's forget about him.

Clara   Twenty years ago . . .

Ella   Oh, you're not going to give me the low-down on the crap that happened in this dump twenty years ago, are you?! I don't need a guided tour of this place, I've a different guided tour in mind . . .

She kisses her. As she does, **Evelyn** *comes back into the kitchen. She coughs.* **Ella** *and* **Clara** *are a little embarrassed.*

Is he all right, Mum?

Evelyn (*to herself*)   Bed and Bedlam! (*Recovering, she examines* **Clara** *and* **Ella**.) What were you two doing when I came in the door?

Ella   Mum . . .

Evelyn   Were you two kissing?

Clara   Mrs Dwyer . . .

Evelyn   Don't Mrs Dwyer me, you lesbian!

Ella   Mum!

Evelyn   Every time I turn my back something funny happens in this Bed and Bugger of a place! First I have your uncle come home to die and then what do I find, my daughter kissing a girl, and let's not forget the other one upstairs about to give birth to a Bed and Bastard, and my husband, wherever he is, the biggest fornicator of all! What did I do to deserve this? The amount of fornication that goes on under this roof! And there's no way to block out the creaking of the beds! Boy, I can tell you, there's nights when I think the house is going to lift off with all the creaking, especially the nights when there's no vacancies and they're all at it at the same time, and there's been quite a few of them, I can tell you. The racket! The bloody racket! The Bed and Bloody racket! And when you think of all the places in this B&B land, full of the same thing, I'm sure them fellas watching from the satellites up in space must be able to hear the whole country creaking from up there! And do you know what I was thinking, with all the fornication that goes on under this roof, I should put in a condom machine in all the bathrooms, now that'd be a first. I mean, we know that's what these Bed and Bastard places are all about so it'd make sense. Yes, that's a good idea, I'll do that, and maybe even get Bord Failte to put in a special mention, all rooms en suite and with condom machines for happy nights of fornication. And isn't that what we fought for all those years ago against the British for, all those heroes giving up their lives to make the country free, so as we could bring up our families the way we wanted! And now look at the country, ruined by the B&B plague! But isn't it a great wee country still, lovely friendly people, big happy smiles, red hair and freckles and crooked teeth, and feet steppin' away to a mighty jig! (*She does a mad jig.*) Oh, begod, begob, begorrah, aren't we the happy people, survived the famine, survived the British, and still able to sing . . . (*She sings an Irish song.*) . . . oh yes, we're a happy B&B land full of creaking beds in the middle of our happy, happy families! And don't get me started on the other noises!

She is now a little out of breath, and is doing her own bit of heavy breathing.

But no, I'm going to kill myself first, amn't I? (*Thinks.*) But not tonight.

She goes to the presses and fridge and starts frantically pulling out everything.

Now, have I enough sausages and rashers for the morning? Have I enough eggs and black pudding? Have I enough cornflakes? Have I enough bread? And what if they want pancakes! What then?

Ella *goes to her.*

Ella   Mum! Mum!

Evelyn   And how about porridge!

Ella *grabs* **Evelyn**'s *hands.*

Ella   Mum, calm down! Sit down!

Evelyn *sits down.*

Evelyn   I'm not joking. One of these days I will kill myself. Just look at me, old before my time. I'm only thirty-eight years of age and I'm an old woman.

Ella   Mum!

Evelyn   Maybe that's what I'll do, start offering myself to the guests, how about that? En suite rooms and the woman of the house thrown in for a little extra. Bed and Brothel, eh! Yes, that's me, the Madam of 'The Bower, Bed and Brothel'! (*Pause.*) But then none of them ever want me. They only have eyes for the daughters. All they ever want from me is an extra roll of toilet paper, or there's pubic hairs in the bath they want removing, or they want their fry-up in olive oil or their pancakes. Pancakes! I bloody well hate making pancakes!

She slams her hand down on the table.

Clara   You're not old, Mrs Dwyer. And you're still beautiful.

Evelyn   Am I?

Clara   I'm sure plenty of the guests have eyes for you as well.

Evelyn   Oh yeh, hope springs eternal, eh?

Silence.

How long?

Ella   What?

Evelyn   This . . . lesbian thing, how long's it been going on?

Clara   A few months.

Evelyn   And what do you do with each other?

Ella   Mum!

Evelyn   At least I suppose you won't end up like the other one with her Bed and Bastard. That's one consolation. (*She looks at* **Ella** *and shakes her head.*) And how do you square it with the Man above? Do you say in your prayers at the end, please, God, forgive me for being a lesbian . . .

Ella   Mum!

Evelyn   Yeh, I know. This is the year whatever it is and we're all supposed to have open minds. But a lesbian . . . where'll that get you? Couldn't you be a solicitor or something? I always wanted you to be a solicitor, dreamt maybe one day you'd be a judge . . . lay down the law, put people in their places for me . . .

Clara   Mrs Dwyer, being gay is not like . . .

Ella   Clara, don't, she knows well what she's saying, she's just winding you up . . .

Evelyn *starts to cry.*

Ella   Mum, Mum, you don't have to worry about me, I'm happy.

Evelyn   I'm not crying about you, it's about something else.

Ella   What, Mum?

Evelyn *stands up.*

Evelyn   I'm going on up. (*To* **Clara**.) Don't keep her up too long.

She is about to go.

Ella   Mum!

Evelyn *stops.* **Ella** *rushes to her, embraces her, and then* **Evelyn** *goes. Silence.*

Ella   God, but she drives me mad sometimes. Sometimes I wish she would just go and kill herself like she's always threatening.

Clara   He killed someone.

Ella   Clara!

Clara   Your mother knows.

Ella   Knows what?

Clara   Who he killed.

Ella   You're getting carried away with yourself, Clara. I suppose you'll be adding this to your guided tours, this'll be the haunted house . . . (*She makes a ghostly sound.*)

The door opens and **Ella** *jumps a little.* **Emer** *comes in. She goes to the fridge. She gets an orange juice and drinks it and then sits down at the table.*

Emer   What was going on down here?

Ella   It was over you.

Emer   No, it wasn't. Just the usual Bed and Bedlam, I'm sure.

Ella   No, it was Bed and Bastard . . .

They look at each other.

So, nearly there.

Emer   Nearly there.

Ella   Your life ruined.

Emer   Says you.

Ella   It's your life.

Emer   Jealous?

Ella   As if.

Emer   You will be.

Ella   Don't count on it.

Emer (*to* **Clara**)   Sisters, eh! Always trying to get one over . . .

Ella   Speak for yourself.

Emer   I am speaking for myself.

Ella   Are you?

Emer   Being pregnant . . . it changes all that.

Ella   Beaten me to it, eh?

Emer   Whatever.

Ella (*looks to* **Clara**)   She's such a mess, really. She's never heard of condoms.

Emer   Maybe I didn't want to use one.

Ella   Wanted to get pregnant, did you?

Emer   Maybe I just did.

Ella   Thought she was getting one over on me, going with that Italian, thought I fancied him, but I didn't. (*She looks to* **Clara**.) And looks where it's gotten her. (*She laughs.*)

Emer   Just can't get a man, can you?

Ella   Can if I want.

Emer   Anyone can get a one-night stand.

Ella   You're proof of that.

Emer   Gianni will come back.

Ella   In your dreams.

Emer   Or maybe I'll go to live in Italy.

Ella   Emer, you're awake, this is not a dream. (*She pinches her.*) You're awake!

Emer   Ow, that hurt!

Ella   She's such a wimp. She was always running to Mammy on me.

Emer   You were a cruel bitch, that's why.

Ella Oh, it's all coming out now, is it?

Emer Who was always hiding my toys on me?

Ella And who was always peeing on my things?

Emer And who was always locking me in presses?

Ella And who was always spitting in my dinner?

Emer And who was always kicking my cat?

Ella And who ripped up my communion dress?

Emer And who made me bite a snail once.

Ella And who put cat shit in my bed?

Emer And who made me eat it then?

Ella And who set fire to my doll's house?

Emer And who cut all my hair off to get me back?

Ella And who gives a shit! Who really gives a shit!

Emer You do!

Ella No, you're the one never forgets anything. If I ever got a sausage that was bigger than the one she got, there'd be tantrums!

Emer See who never forgets anything! That only happened the once! What date did that happen on? I bet you remember!

Ella See who doesn't remember! See who doesn't remember!

They scowl at each other.

She did burn down my doll's house. Stuffed it with newspapers and up it went. Lucky she didn't burn down the whole house.

Emer Yeh, you were there to tell on me, weren't you?

Ella Well, lucky I was!

Emer *suddenly turns around and screams.* **Owen** *is standing in the doorway.*

Owen   She's gone to bed, has she?

Ella   Who? Mum?

Ella *nods. Suddenly* **Emer** *gets a twinge.*

Emer   Oh, my God! Oh, my God!

Ella   Is it starting?

Emer   I don't know, I don't know!

It subsides and **Emer** *relaxes and sits down.*

Emer   God, I can't wait till this is all over.

Ella   You nearly did it there, Uncle Owen, scaring her like that. The baby'd be weeks early.

Owen *looks around.*

Ella   Uncle Owen?

Owen *picks up the deck of cards and starts dealing them, creating two hands. He sits down and picks up one of the hands. The three women look at him.*

Clara   Is one of us supposed to play with you?

Owen *shakes his head.*

Clara   Who's the other hand for then?

Ella   You are awake this time, aren't you, Uncle Owen?

Owen   It's just . . . sometimes . . . the yoke . . . (*Points to his head.*) . . . makes me do things . . . say things . . . it's like having a swarm of bluebottles in my head buzzing about like mad.

The sound of a foghorn. He puts the cards down.

Owen   As a boy I always wanted to be the man in the lighthouse. He was a hero, he was a god. He suffered out there to make sure we could all sleep safely in our beds . . .

he moaned with the pain every so often . . . and then the
light would sweep past my window and I'd know it was safe
to head off into the darkness of sleep, I'd be safe from the
creatures that roamed there . . .

*He picks up the cards again and shakes his head and then throws his
hand in.*

One day we rowed out there, your mother and me. We stole
a boat, belonging to Benny Maguire. Your mother, she
always had the bit of the devil in her, and she put me up to
it. We didn't speak on the way, the only sound, the
splashing of the oars into the water. But as we got closer to
the rock, I started to get scared. What awaited us? What
would he be like, the man in the lighthouse? Would we even
see him? We banged up against the rocks and I scrambled
out to tie up the boat and help Evelyn out. At first we just
hid out there among the rocks, looking up at the towering
building. Then we gradually got our courage back and we
crept off the rocks and it was the funniest thing ever, there
was a vegetable patch, and a lawn neatly bordered with
flowers just beyond that leading up to a door. He was
obviously a gardener! (*He laughs.*) There were potatoes,
cabbages, cauliflowers, carrots and whatnot! I pulled a
carrot and cleaned it and I bit into it. I was thirsty after all
the rowing, and it tasted so good. Then we crept towards
the building. To the door. We looked it up and down.
There was a knocker. Evelyn was all up for banging it but I
had to stop her, he'd be sleeping, the man in the lighthouse,
I said, and we wrestled over that knocker. (*He laughs.*) We fell
on to the lawn then and spread ourselves out and it was like
lying out in God's garden, the most perfect rest you could
imagine. (*Silence.*) Evelyn got bored and started tickling me
and the sun was sinking towards the horizon so I knew it
was time to go, even though I didn't want to. We crept back
to the boat and I rowed us back to the shore and as we got
out of the boat I could hear Evelyn sobbing quietly in the
darkness. She wanted to stay too. (*Pause.*) Later we heard
Benny Maguire was going round the village threatening

everyone with murder for stealing his boat. (*Smiles.*) Oh yes, your mother had a bit of the devil in her.

Ella   Clara's father, he was a lighthouse man. He would've been the man in the lighthouse. Did he do gardening, Clara?

Clara   Yeh, it was his pride and joy. But there's no one out there any more.

Owen (*almost to himself*)   There's still someone out there.

Emer *has another spasm and she cries out loudly, but relaxes again. She tries to get up.*

Emer   Any chance of a hand here, big sis.

Ella   Oh, you want my help now, do you?

Emer   I'm going to make you an aunt, you should be grateful.

Ella   Can't wait.

Ella *helps her out the door.* **Owen** *continues to play cards.*

Clara   Will I play with you?

Owen   No.

Clara   Are you waiting for someone?

Owen *looks at her.*

Owen   Your father was the lighthouse man.

Owen *looks up at her, then back at his cards.*

Clara   There's still someone out there, on the lighthouse, you said. What did you mean?

Owen   Still someone . . . yes, before . . .

Owen *looks at her.*

Clara   Who? Who is it?

Owen   He saw. He saw everything. The man in the lighthouse.

Clara   Saw what? You can tell me . . .

Ella *comes back in and* **Clara** *is a little disappointed.*

Owen   I've enough of playing cards. (*He nods.*) It's time.

He stands up and goes out the side door. **Ella** *goes to the door.*

Ella   Uncle Owen! Uncle Owen, where are you going? Uncle Owen! (*To* **Clara**.) Where's he going at this hour? Oh, do I give a shit!

Clara *goes to her at the door.* **Ella** *closes the door and sits down at the table.*

Ella   He didn't say where he was going?

Clara   No.

Ella   I hope he doesn't drop dead when he's out.

She goes to the table and picks up one hand of cards. Then she picks up the other hand and hands it to **Clara**.

Play!

They sit down. They each throw down cards.

Ella   Three for me.

Clara   Three for me as well.

Ella *deals cards.*

Clara   I love you, Ella.

Ella *looks at her cards, rearranging them.*

Ella   What've you got?

Clara   Ella, did you hear me? I love you.

Ella   I heard you the first time, yeh.

She puts her cards down.

Two pair, ace high. What've you got?

Clara   Two pair, king high.

Ella   I win.

Clara (*quietly*)   I lose.

Ella *laughs and screeches. She throws her arms around* **Clara**.

Ella   Let's play again. I like winning.

Someone enters the kitchen and they are startled. It is **Lotte**.

Lotte   I cannot sleep. I cannot sleep in this house. It is terrible when I cannot sleep. It is not a very quiet house. I will have to ask for my money back tomorrow.

The sound of the foghorn.

Act Three

Evelyn *runs in to the cooker and grabs the frying pan.*

Evelyn   Bed and Bugger! Just a little burnt, and if they complain it'll be World War Three, I can tell you that now, you little buggers!

She puts sausages and rashers on a plate and rushes out with it. The door opens and **Owen** *comes in from outside dragging a sack. He sits down at the table.* **Evelyn** *comes rushing back in.*

Up already? I'll get you your breakfast in a minute.

Owen *settles the bag at his feet like it was a pet.*

Evelyn   Bloody Germans! The cheek! Complaining about a little burnt on the sausages after all the frying they've done!

She rushes out again. **Owen** *shakes the sack and looks at it as he speaks.*

Owen   She's still looking well, isn't she? You could tell from an early age she was going to be a beauty! From the time she started to grow (*Gestures, indicating breasts.*) . . . they had to be beaten back.

Evelyn *rushes back in.*

Evelyn   More toast! More tea! Boy, they're really putting it away this morning! And the amount of butter they're getting through, laying it on like we get it for free from the EU butter mountain or something!

She puts bread in the toaster and pours water into a teapot. She pours **Owen** *a cup and then rushes out with the pot.*

Owen   And when I started going out with Annie O'Dea, she was jealous. Wouldn't speak to me for a week. Then she got over it, and the questions started. What did we talk about, what did we do? I'd tell her some things, others I wouldn't. She was too young. Not that me and Annie

O'Dea got up to much, I was sixteen, she was fifteen, but she was some kisser!

Evelyn *comes back in, grabs the toast and rushes back out.*

Owen (*laughs*)   Like the wind she is! (*Pause.*) She was a flyer then as well, running everywhere, her hair and dress flying behind her! (*Laughs.*) One day when Annie and me were walking along the beach, I saw her flying over the headland, and I knew she'd been following us, spying on us, the little rascal.

He shakes the bag. **Evelyn** *comes rushing back in and sits down at the table for a moment. She looks around and listens.*

Evelyn   I must've gotten all the bluebottles.

She listens again, then looks to **Owen***.*

I'll have a cup of tea with you when I get this lot out of the way.

She gets up and puts some more toast on and goes out. **Owen** *reaches into the bag and takes out a skull and places it on the table.*

Owen   But it didn't last long between me and Annie O'Dea, anyway, and that made her happy. Then she had me all to herself again. We were very close, you see, because our parents, well, they didn't get on very well, always arguing, you know the kind of thing.

He follows this with other bones. **Evelyn** *rushes in, grabs toast and rushes out again.* **Owen** *has stopped, but now he places the rest of the bones on the table.* **Evelyn** *comes back in with a load of dishes and places them in the sink. She puts the kettle on, then starts washing the dishes.*

Evelyn   So, what'll you have for breakfast, Owen?

Owen   I don't know. I'm not much of one for breakfast. I'm happy enough with a cup of tea most of the time.

Evelyn I could make you pancakes. I wouldn't mind making you pancakes. You must eat them over there all the time.

Owen No, no. Never touched them. Too fattening.

Evelyn You used to love scrambled eggs, didn't you?

Owen I did.

Evelyn Maybe I'll make you scrambled eggs as a treat.

She turns to him, sees the skeleton, and turns back to what she was doing. She stops, then slowly turns again and screams, then stifles it.

Owen, Owen, what's that on the table?

Owen *doesn't answer.* **Evelyn** *moves slowly to the table.*

Evelyn Owen, Owen, where did you get that from?

Owen I dug him up.

Lotte *appears in the door.*

Lotte Mrs Dwyer.

Evelyn *turns in shock and rushes to the door to block her view.*

Evelyn Yes, what is it?

Lotte I didn't sleep very well last night and I think I should get some of my money back.

Evelyn Do you now?

Lotte Yes, I do. And it is because of him. (*Points to* **Owen**.) He did not die last night. (*Pause.*) I did not sleep.

Evelyn *reaches into her pocket and hands her some money.*

Evelyn There you are now, love, that's been burning a hole in my pocket all day, I was going to put it in the poor box for the starving babies in Africa, but sure, you take it!

Lotte That is very good of you.

Lotte *goes and* **Evelyn** *turns in horror to* **Owen** *and the table.*

Evelyn   Owen, get it out of my kitchen.

Owen   I did a good job when I buried him, I could hardly find the spot myself. There's no garden there any more. Where the lawn was is tarmac for the helicopter and the vegetable patch is just weeds.

Silence.

Evelyn   Owen, what is it, and why is it in my kitchen?

Owen   It's 'him'.

Evelyn   Him?

Owen   'Him'.

Evelyn   Who's 'him'?

Owen   You know who 'him' is.

Evelyn   No, I don't.

Owen   Yes, you do, Evelyn.

Evelyn   'Him'?

Owen   Yes, 'him'.

Evelyn (*exasperated*)   I still don't know who 'him' is!

Owen   'Him' is 'him'.

Evelyn   What kind of gibberish is 'him' is 'him'?!

Owen   You remember 'him'.

Evelyn   How can I remember 'him' when I don't know who 'him' is?! Now, get 'him' off my kitchen table.

Owen   'Him' the hymn singer. (*He laughs to himself.*)

Evelyn *sits down at the table.*

Evelyn   Owen, you're not well. (*Pause.*) Now, let's put him back . . .

She grabs the sack, but he stops her.

Owen   Evelyn, leave him be.

He lifts up the skull and stares at it.

The day I saw him first driving about in his car, the big broad grin on him, the wave he had on him like he was the Pope! Father Molloy. (*Pause.*) Father Molloy. (*Pause.*) Father Molloy.

Evelyn   Father Molloy.

Owen   'Him' . . .

Evelyn   Father Molloy.

Owen   . . . the hymn singer.

Evelyn   You, you, you . . .

She strikes the skull.

Owen   The way he'd come knocking at the door, rubbing his hands, and his 'May God be with you all under this roof'.

Evelyn   You, you, you . . .

She strikes the skull again.

Owen   You were only thirteen when he called first.

Evelyn   You, you, you . . . fucker!

Up above we see **Clara**, *over the set, looking down into it.*

Clara   The morning after I came across Owen Quinn for the first time, I remembered the story about the priest who'd disappeared off the face of the earth some twenty years ago. At the time everyone went along with the theory he'd just run away. They helped look for him, half-heartedly, all knowing full well that one among them had killed him. For a few weeks it was the talk of the country, and the rumour mill ran riot. Some said he'd run off with a woman and didn't ever want to be found again and was living under an assumed name in a quiet corner of the country. One woman said she'd heard him talk of going to Valparaiso in Chile.

Another man thought he went off to the Missions in the Far East to save the black babies. Someone else said he was working in a leper colony in India. But no trace was found of him, no word, no call, no letter ever received from him again. And his mother and two sisters came to help look for him and they put up missing posters and for months the new priest that replaced him said prayers. But after some months his mother had to give up the search and the missing posters faded and then were blown or worn away . . . but it was only when I met Ella's uncle that I connected it with the story my father told me about a man who rowed out to the rock one night under the crescent moon and rowed away again with the rising sun, leaving something behind. He told that story to me more than once, and I always knew it had some dark significance . . .

Evelyn *is about to strike the skull again when they hear the door opening slowly.* **Evelyn** *quickly grabs the bag and clears the skeleton away but for one bone.* **Emer** *comes in the door.*

Evelyn   Hi, love.

Emer   Oh, Mum, I'm fed up going around like a stuffed turkey, I'm really fed up.

Evelyn *lunges, grabs the bone and puts it away in the sack.*

Emer   What was that?

Evelyn   What was what? (*Quickly.*) What do you want for breakfast?

Emer   Just a cup of tea, Mum.

Evelyn *pours her a cup of tea.*

Emer   I had the weirdest dream, Mum. (*Pause.*) I dreamt I gave birth to a skeleton.

Evelyn   Skeleton? There's no skeletons in this house!

Emer   I dreamt it, Mum!

Owen   Is that your doing?

He shakes the bag. **Evelyn** *gives him an angry look.*

Emer   I'm not making it up, Mum, I just woke up, I just had the dream.

Evelyn   That's normal, I had the craziest dreams when I was pregnant as well.

Emer   Mum . . . I'm scared . . .

Evelyn   It's only a dream and dreams never come true as I know only too well!

Owen   You're playing tricks on us all.

Evelyn (*to* **Owen**)   Would you like to take that bag of sticks out back, Owen. Owen went out to collect sticks for a fire. He finds it cold here after living in Las Vegas for so long. He used to love doing that as a boy, didn't you, Owen? Collecting sticks. You can take them out back, Owen.

Owen *doesn't answer.*

Evelyn   Owen!

She grabs the bag, but he holds on to it, and he won't let go.

Evelyn   Owen, take the bag out back.

Owen   'May God be with you all under this roof.'

Evelyn (*weakly*)   Owen, stop, and take the bag out back.

Owen *doesn't move.* **Evelyn** *buries her face in her hands, as if she were crying.*

Emer   What is it, Mum?

Evelyn   Oh, I was just thinking about when I got pregnant first . . .

Owen *shakes the bag.*

Owen   'May God be with you all under this roof.'

Evelyn (*recovering*)   We weren't married, you see, me and your father, and it was all a bit sudden.

Owen (*loudly*)   'May God be with you all under this roof'.

Evelyn (*snapping*)   Owen!

Emer   I miss Dad, Mum.

Ella *comes into the kitchen, looking very sleepy.*

Ella   What's for breakfast, Mum?

Evelyn *doesn't answer, and starts to cry again.*

Evelyn   I know you do, love.

Ella   What?

Evelyn   I'm talking to your sister.

Ella   What's wrong with her?

Emer   I miss Dad.

Ella *makes a dismissive sound.*

Emer   Do you never miss, Dad?

Ella   Who needs men, fathers, husbands, they're dispensable.

Emer   I'll get Gianni back. When the baby is born, I'll take him to Italy . . .

Ella   And they'll roll out the red carpet, and take you to meet the pope!

Ella *shakes her head.* **Owen** *shakes the bag.*

Ella   Where did you go last night, Uncle Owen?

Owen   'May God be with you all under this roof.'

Ella   Amen.

Owen   Then in you came, and sat there drinking our tea, your eye on us all.

Ella   Who, Uncle Owen?

Owen   Your eye!

Evelyn (*pouring her tea*)   You'll have scrambled eggs, won't you, Owen? And, Emer, you'll have some as well, you must be hungry. And, Ella, what about you?

Ella   Where did you go last night, Uncle Owen. We were worried about you.

Evelyn *breaks eggs into a bowl, keeping an eye on* **Owen**. **Ella** *looks to* **Evelyn**, *then to* **Owen**. **Owen** *reaches into the bag and takes out the skull and places it on the table. He follows with other bones.* **Emer** *looks at this in horror.* **Ella** *blesses herself.* **Evelyn** *is rooted to the spot.* **Emer** *looks as if she is going to have a fit.* **Evelyn** *goes to her.*

Emer   Mum! Mum!

Evelyn   It's OK, love, it's not real.

Ella *watches* **Owen** *place the rest of the bones on the table.* **Emer** *starts to hyperventilate and gasps for air.*

Evelyn   It's OK, love, it's only one of Uncle Owen's jokes. I'll bring you upstairs.

Evelyn *helps* **Emer** *up and out of the kitchen.* **Ella** *and* **Owen** *look at the skeleton in silence.*

Ella   You killed him, didn't you? Clara was right. (*Pause.*) You killed someone, didn't you, Uncle Owen? And that's him . . .

Owen   I went knocking at his door in the middle of the night. Down he came thinking someone must be dying, that he was being called to adminster the last rites, and in I stepped, blubbering out of me, and then it happened. I grabbed him, yes, I grabbed him, and I don't know what came over me, I meant to give him a good hiding, I think that's what I meant to do, but my hands, they took over, and they went for his neck, maybe that's what I intended to do all day, maybe I was only fooling myself on the way that he was in for a good hiding, but my hands, they were around his neck. He was strong, but not stronger than me. Rowing makes your hands and arms strong, and at that time I was fairly handy at the rowing. When I was done, I dragged him down to the point, got him into a boat and rowed him out to the lighthouse where I buried him. I sat there till sun up trying to say prayers, prayers for him, prayers for me, but not an amen would pass my lips, and then I rowed back, the sun rising in a blaze behind me. A more beautiful morning I never remember.

Silence.

Ella   Who was he?

Owen   Father Molloy.

Ella   Yes, but who was Fatherr Molloy?

Evelyn *comes back in the door. Silence.*

Evelyn   Haven't you put that away yet?

Ella   Uncle Owen just told me how he killed . . . Father Molloy.

Evelyn *gasps.*

Evelyn   He did no such thing, he's only making all that up, it's his tumour.

Ella   Who is he?

The doorbell rings. No one moves. The doorbell again.

Ella   Mum, there's someone at the door.

Evelyn   I don't care.

The doorbell again.

Ella   Mum!

Evelyn *doesn't move. Silence.* **Evelyn** *moves to the table to grab the skull.*

Owen (*emphatically*)   Leave him there!

The doorbell rings again. A man, **Hannes***, appears at the guest door.*

Hannes   Hello, Evelyn, can we have more of toast?

Evelyn *moves to block his view.*

Evelyn   Yes, of course, Herr Kippenhan.

Hannes   You can call me Hannes, Evelyn.

Evelyn   Hannes.

The doorbell rings again.

Hannes   And your doorbell is ringing all the time.

Evelyn   Yes, thank you.

Hannes   Thank you, you're welcome. You were very good to give Lotte back money. Lotte is a very bad sleeper . . .

Evelyn   Yes, yes, yes . . .

She ushers him back out the guest door, and then closes it. The doorbell rings again.

(*Shouts.*) Will you stop ringing that doorbell!

She gets weak and sits down at the table.

Owen   In the weeks after, with the search on, I wanted to shout it out: I did it! I killed him! So many times, so many times until I knew I had to leave. I'd've gone earlier, but then everyone might know. Everyone might guess it was me and the why of it, with Evelyn getting married and everything.

Evelyn   Owen!

Ella   Who is he?

Evelyn   He was a bad man. Did bad things . . .

Ella   Why did *you* kill him, Uncle Owen? Did he do something to you?

Owen   Not to me.

Ella   Who is he?

Evelyn (*shouts*)   Will you stop asking that!

Ella   Did he do something to you, Mum?

Evelyn   He did nothing to me.

Ella   Who is he, Uncle Owen?

Evelyn   He was a priest. Father Molloy was his name.

Ella   Who is he, Uncle Owen?

Evelyn   I've already told you who he was!

Ella   Who is he, Uncle Owen?

Owen   He's your father.

Silence.

Ella (*to skull*)   Hi, Dad!

Evelyn *covers her face with her hands. She is sobbing heavily.*

Evelyn   Oh, Owen, you shouldn't've told her that. I'm sorry, honey, I never wanted you to find out.

Evelyn *cries even more.*

Owen   She was only sixteen. (*Faintly.*) One day . . . she was flying over the headland . . . the little rascal! And then . . .

Ella *looks at* **Owen**.

Ella   So my father is a perverted old priest.

Evelyn *recovers a little and looks at* **Ella**.

Evelyn   Aren't you upset?

Ella   No.

Evelyn (*bursting out crying*)   What kind of a daughter did I bring up at all?

Silence.

Ella (*to skull*)   So, you're my real dad.

Evelyn   Don't call him that! Don't call him that!

Ella   But he is my real dad.

There is a knock at the back door and **Clara** *walks in.* **Evelyn** *dives on to the skeleton to try and cover it up, and tries to look casual.*

Clara   Hi!

Ella   Hi!

Evelyn   Get out of my house, you lesbian!

Ella   Mum!

Evelyn   Get her out!

Clara *comes closer and looks at the skeleton under* **Evelyn**.

Clara   I know who he is. Father Bill Molloy is his name. He disappeared over twenty years ago.

Slowly **Evelyn** *gets off the table.* **Owen** *adjusts the position of the skull.*

Owen   I did feel sorry for his mother, as she went from door to door asking everyone about his movements, his last ones. She called to our house and I wanted to tell her why I'd killed you, but her jaded eyes stopped me.

A knock at the door and **Hannes** *appears at the hall door.*

Hannes   Excuse me, Evelyn.

Evelyn *rushes to him, to blind his view.*

Evelyn   Yes, Hannes.

Hannes   The toilet in the room is blocked. I wonder can someone do something.

Evelyn   Of course, Hannes, anything for you.

Hannes   You're welcome.

Evelyn *ushers him out and closes the door.*

Evelyn (*to herself*)   If you didn't shite so much . . . too much brown bread, I knew it! I just knew it! Oh, that'll be a lovely job for me later!

Emer *comes back in.*

Emer   Mum!

Evelyn (*shouts*)   What?

Emer   Mum, I'm scared!

Clara *hugs* **Ella**. *The doorbell rings again.*

Evelyn (*shouts*)   Will someone get the door!

Emer (*shouts*)   I'll get it!

Emer *goes out. A knock on the guest door.* **Evelyn** *rushes to it to hold it closed. She looks around.*

Evelyn   And a bluebottle, just when I can't . . .

Owen   'May God be with you all under this roof.'

The doorbell rings again. **Evelyn** *looks around desperately, then picks up the swatter and swats once vigorously.*

Evelyn   That's it! I've had enough! I can't take this any more! I've had it up to here with this Bed and Bastard of a place! I've had enough of you all! I'm going to kill myself! I should've done it a long time ago! I was going to kill myself when I found out, when I found out I was in the family way! (*Laughs derisively.*) I even had the noose made up, but I didn't like the thought of that! So I went down to the point and I was going to drown myself. For a whole week I tried, every day I got into the gap down there, but I couldn't do it! Now, I'm ready for it! Bed and Breakfast! No more!

She rushes out the door. **Ella** *and* **Clara** *look at each other.*

Clara   Is she serious?

Ella   No.

Clara   She sounded like she was. Ella, I think we should go after her.

Ella   Oh, she's always flying off the handle like that.

Clara   Ella!

Ella *and* **Clara** *are about to go, but* **Owen** *grabs* **Ella**.

Owen   She was so beautiful when she was sixteen. There's photographs, but they don't do her justice. (*He stands up and grabs* **Ella**.) You look so like her. She was so, so, so beautiful. And to think that he, that he . . .

Ella   Uncle Owen, you're hurting me!

Ella *loosens his grip.*

Clara   Ella, come on!

Clara *and* **Ella** *exit.*

Owen   I'd watch her go off to meet her friends, and I felt so proud, because I knew my sister would stand out. She was the pick of the bunch. Every boy in the village had an eye for her, and all my friends would ask about her, letting their intentions be known. (*Pause. He smiles.*) She was friendly with Eddie Dwyer, and she told me she liked him, and one evening she asked me if she should kiss him. I didn't know what to say. That evening when she came home, she smiled at me and rushed up the stairs to bed, and I felt so happy. To know she'd had her first kiss. (*Pause.*) Her first kiss.

He looks at the skeleton and we see the tension in his hands again.

Act Four

Night. A cliff formation The sound of waves. **Clara** *rushes on through the rocks and looks about.* **Ella** *follows after her and sits down.*

Ella   Why do you care, she's my mother, let her drown herself. Bed and Bedone with it! It's dark, we'll never find her now. We've spent the whole day on a wild goose chase and I'm knackered.

Clara *continues to look about.*

Ella   Oh, I get it, I get it now, you fancy my mother, don't you? You're only with me to get closer to her, aren't you? Bed and Betrayal, isn't that it?

Clara *comes back to* **Ella**.

Clara   You know, you're turning into your mother already.

Ella   I'm not. I am not!

Clara   You are!

Ella *grabs* **Clara** *and starts kissing her.* **Clara** *pushes her off.*

Clara   Ella, not now, we're looking for your mother.

Ella   Why do you care so much?

Clara   I don't want her to die, do I?

Ella   And you're your father's daughter. The lighthouse man's daughter. You'll keep the world safe, and turn into a nutcase wandering the cliffs like your old man.

Clara   This is where he used to come all the time and sit looking out at . . . he was lost after they automated it . . . he spent thirty-odd years out there.

Ella   He died for that lighthouse, eh?

Clara   Only one boat was lost in his whole time out there. The *Mary Ann.* I was seven. (*Pause.*) Everyone up here was on their knees praying. They tried to get the lifeboat out there, but they were beaten back again and again. And for a long time it seemed the *Mary Ann* would just ride it out, not be driven against the cliffs or against the rocks around the lighthouse. Then you could hear the prayers getting louder, no longer lost in the wind and the rain, and it seemed the storm was easing off, when a great cry went up, as the *Mary Ann* seemed to dip dangerously, and then all of a sudden it just disappeared under the waves.

She looks about again.

Come on, Ella, we've got to keep looking!

She leaves.

Ella   Bed and Bedamned! I'm buggered if I'm going to spend the rest of the night following her. She's my mother, not hers. (*Shakes her head.*) Bed and Bugger!

Clara *comes back in.*

Clara   Aren't you coming?

Ella *goes to her, and sits beside her.*

Ella   I'm a priest's daughter. Now I know why she didn't want me to make my Holy Communion. The fight I fought for that white dress. And to spite her afterwards I learnt the catechism inside out. And when I was done with that, I turned to the Bible till I knew a lot of it by heart. What a waste! Isn't that sad? It must've driven her mad. And I gave Emer a tough time, I can tell you. Mum didn't hardly touch me at all when I was a kid. I'd see her hug Emer and think: Emer has to be hugged, and I'd hug her too. But did anyone hug me?

Clara *hugs her.* **Evelyn** *appears, but when she sees* **Clara** *and* **Ella**, *she hides.*

Ella   Too late.

Clara   Too late? (*Looks at her.*) Ella, do you love me?

Ella   'Course I do.

Clara   Do you? Sometimes I think you're with me to get back at your mother.

Ella   I don't do everything in my life just to spite her.

Clara   No?

Ella   No. (*Smiles.*) You make me feel safe.

Clara   Is that it?

Ella   And I like the way you tell about things like the *Mary Ann*. And you're a ride.

Clara laughs. *Then she looks at* **Ella** *for a moment, before looking about again.*

Clara   Come on, Ella!

Ella   She won't drown herself, I know her well.

Clara   She never ran off like this before, did she?

Ella   No, but . . . she was always threatening to.

Clara   Ella, come on!

Ella   She'll never do it!

Clara *goes, followed by* **Ella**. **Evelyn** *appears.*

Evelyn   See if I won't drown myself! I will! But I'm going to wait a few minutes yet. I'm out of breath. I'll just sit down here for a few minutes, then I'll get on with it.

She sits down where **Clara** *sat, the spot where* **Clara** *said her father always used to sit.*

Here you go again, talking to yourself, because no one listens, no one gives a damn. Where did I ever get such ungrateful daughters? (*Nods her head.*) I know, I know. One from a fornicating priest and the other from a fornicating bastard!

Owen   Evelyn, is that you?

Owen *appears and startles her.*

Evelyn   Oh, you! And I thought you were . . . someone come to ravish a maiden in distress!

She looks out at the lighthouse.

Owen   Do you remember, Evelyn, the day we rowed out there, when we were children. We didn't do anything, just hid for a while, looked the place over, ate one of the carrots, and then sunned ourselves on the lawn. If only we could've stayed out there for ever, eh?

Evelyn   But we couldn't've lived on carrots all our lives. And look at the life I've had. I wouldn't want to have missed that for anything! I look around the kitchen sometimes and I get jealous of the bluebottles. The easy life they have!

She looks at **Owen**.

And children, they never turn out the way you plan it. They get their own ideas . . . (*Shakes her head.*) . . . just to spite us, isn't that right?

Owen   I wouldn't know, Evelyn.

Evelyn   You have two like me, and you think they'll get on like a house on fire, but they end up hating the sight of each other. I tried my best with them, but they were a handful . . . oh, if only I was a bluebottle and somebody would just swat me into kingdom come!

Owen   Evelyn . . .

He looks out at the lighthouse.

Owen   Evelyn . . . Evelyn . . . you came home and I knew something was wrong and I thought Eddie Dwyer was after doing something to you, but you said you'd been at choir practice. Well, I said, choir practice can't be that bad, and I thought maybe you'd sang very badly and I left it at that, but that night when I was on my way to bed I heard you crying and I knocked and went in and then you told me . . .

Evelyn (*getting angry*)   And you would come home to die! Couldn't you have done your dying over there and left me in peace?! Well now, I'm off to do my own bit of dying!

Evelyn *rushes off and* **Owen** *watches her for a few moments.*

Owen   Evelyn . . . Evelyn . . .

Ella *rushes on.*

Ella   Uncle Owen! We still haven't found her.

Owen   She was just here.

Ella   She was just here! Why didn't you hold on to her! Which way did she go?

Owen *points.* **Ella** *looks, seems about to run, but then sits down.*

Ella   Oh, I'm fed up. Let her drown herself, she'd be doing us all a favour.

She sits down again.

Boy, Uncle Owen, you've really stirred the shit. Suppose it was the best thing for you to leave here then. Had to go, I suppose, to get away from it all, leave it all behind, eh? But I'm glad you killed my dad. He had it coming, didn't he?

Owen   The day I left for America, I thought I was leaving it all behind. I thought I was leaving him behind. As we flew out over the Atlantic, I felt totally free. I closed my eyes and started to imagine what my new life was going to be like . . . but all I could see was his face, with my hands around his throat. (*Pause.*) When I got to New York, I thought that'd be gone, but I kept seeing it everywhere, his face . . . in reflections in shop windows, in mirrors. Then I thought if I got away from the coast, far away from the coast, he'd be gone. So one day I took a Greyhound bus and set off for Las Vegas. I thought I'd try my luck out there, I was always good at poker and things. And I was sure I'd done it, I was sure he was gone, but we were only a mile out on to the highway when I looked out the window and caught a reflection again. I knew then he'd be with me for life . . . yes, I was a lifer . . .

Silence.

Ella   And did you never meet a woman, get married or anything?

Owen   There was one . . . Gayle . . . (*He stops.*) . . .

Ella   And?

Owen   I could've been happy with her . . . but he never let me be happy . . .

He looks about.

She was pregnant . . . but that didn't work out . . . and we never recovered from that. (*He shouts.*) Did we? Did we? Did we? (*He stops, then looks at* **Ella**, *and says quietly:*) Did we?

Ella   That's sad. (*Smiles.*) We always imagined you being a big gambler out in Las Vegas, living the high life.

Owen   I was a doorman most of the time, that's what I did.

Ella   Someone has to open doors, I suppose. And Gayle, tell me about her. Was she a showgirl or something?

Owen   She worked in bars in hotels.

Ella   Someone has to pour the drinks as well, I suppose. (*Giggles.*) Me and Emer always pictured you driving around in the big limos and wearing huge ten-gallon hats and with a woman on each arm.

Clara *comes in.*

Clara   There you are.

Ella   She was here, and Owen let her go. At least we know she's not dead yet.

Clara *looks about.*

Clara   I can see a fog starting to roll in. It'll be harder to find her . . .

Ella   Well, the lighthouse'll come on, that'll keep her safe, won't it?

Clara *once again sits on the spot where her father used to sit.* **Owen** *leans in to* **Ella**.

Owen   I have no regrets . . . about what I did. Evelyn was only a little girl . . .

Ella   She was sixteen, wasn't she?

Owen   Yes, yes . . . but she was innocent. (*Pause.*) I'd be playing roulette and the wheel'd turn and in the spinning I'd see his face, but I knew I'd done the right thing, I'd done what had to be done. He destroyed her . . . ruined her life.

Ella   Seems more like he ruined yours, Uncle Owen.

Owen   My life . . . doesn't amount to much, you're right there. But I have that one thing I did that I can look back on and say, I did what had to be done. That's enough . . .

Ella   Is it?

Owen   Oh, yes . . .

He looks at his hands.

I'd've done anything for my little sister . . . anything . . .

Evelyn *appears.*

Evelyn   Well, isn't this nice? And I thought you were all out here looking for me!

Ella   We gave up.

Evelyn   That's the thanks you get. What were you all expecting to get, a grandstand view from up here?

Ella   We're waiting for it to start.

Evelyn   I'm not going to do it when it suits you.

Ella   Suit yourself.

Evelyn   I will. Do you hear that, Owen? That's the gratitude you get for years and years of slaving away bringing up children. They don't care if you live or die. Well, I'm going to become a martyr tonight, how do you like that? A martyr for all women!

Ella   We could do with a new martyr.

Evelyn   That's settled then.

Ella   Before you do kill yourself, I wanted to ask you one question. (*Pause.*) Did Dad . . . Eddie know?

Evelyn   Know what?

Ella   He wasn't my real dad.

Evelyn   He was always an innocent abroad.

Ella   You tricked him.

Evelyn   He was always on about marrying me, from the first time I met him. Once I knew . . . Oh, I don't have to answer your questions.

Ella   He found out, didn't he, isn't that it?

Evelyn   Found out what?

Ella   Found out what! That he wasn't my father.

Evelyn   I don't have to listen to this.

Clara   Of course he found out.

Evelyn   What would you know, you're not part of our family, in fact, you're not part of the human race, are you?

Ella   Don't you go insulting Clara like that! She's my girlfriend!

Evelyn *slaps her and* **Ella** *jumps at her, and they fight.*

Ella   I hate you! I hate you!

Evelyn   And I hate you!

Ella   You always did, and now at least I know why.

Evelyn   Well, that's good!

Ella   Why didn't you go to England instead of having me!

Evelyn   I should've. That's what I should've done, and if I'd known anything, that's what I would've done!

Ella   I hate you!

Evelyn   And I hate you!

They struggle even more. **Clara** *helps pull them apart, and* **Evelyn** *and* **Ella** *end up sprawled on the ground.*

That's the last straw, my own daughter attacking me! Now I'll show you! Just see if I don't drown myself!

She gets up and runs out.

Clara   Ella, come on, we better go after her.

Ella   No way!

Clara   Ella!

Ella   Why don't you go, Uncle Owen, if you say you'd do anything for her. And, anyway, it's all your fault, coming home and digging up my dad like that!

Owen *stays sitting.*

Clara   Ella, come on!

Ella   Kiss me first.

Clara (*quietly*)   No . . . not here . . . (*She looks around at the spot where her father used to sit.*)

Ella   Kiss me.

Clara   Ella, this is where my dad died.

Ella *kisses her.* **Clara** *slaps her.* **Ella** *slaps her back.*

Clara   Thanks, I needed that.

The sound of the foghorn.

Now, let's go!

Ella   Uncle Owen, we're going to go after her.

Clara   There's that fog rolling in off the sea now. Before long everything'll be covered up . . .

They leave.

Owen   Oh no, nothing'll be covered up again, nothing . . .

He holds out his hands.

Not a day I spent over there I didn't think about you . . . (*His hands get more tense.*) . . . that look in your eyes . . . the look of welcome . . . as if you'd been waiting for me . . . waiting for someone to come . . .

His hands stretch and he seems to wrestle with something. Then his hands turn in on themselves and he seems to break down inwardly, his hands still tense. **Hannes** *comes on, in hiking gear.*

Hannes   Hello. Hello. It is a nice evening.

He holds out his hand and starts to shake **Owen**'s *hand vigorously.*

It is a nice evening for a long walk. My name is Hannes. I'm from Stuttgart in Germany. I am staying in the Bed and Breakfast. 'The Bower'. It is over there. You know what means 'Bower'? I looked up in the dictionary. It can mean a dwelling, a cottage. Or a shady place, an arbour. Or a bedroom, a boudoir, as the French they say. I think boudoir is very interesting, don't you. Why it is called 'The Bower', I am wondering? (*Looks.*) I have seen you before? Are you at 'The Bower' as well?

He lets **Owen**'s *hand go and starts to take in very deep breaths.*

It is a very nice evening. A very lot of fresh air. My wife is in the bed. She doesn't sleep very well in the night. I become the blame all the time. If I breathe she cannot sleep. But it is nice to become the fresh air without her.

He sees something.

What is that? What does that woman? Is she a mad woman? I think she must be needing help. You must come and help me.

Hannes *runs off.* **Owen** *gets to his knees and stretches out his hands. As he does,* **Lotte** *appears.*

Lotte   Hello.

Owen   Hello.

Lotte   I am looking for a man.

Owen   Oh.

Lotte (*laughing*)   Oh nein, no, no, no, I do not mean that looking. (*Looks at* **Owen**.) But you are also staying in the Bed and Breakfast. Yes, you are the crazy man who is possessed and is going to die! How does it feel? Oh, that is not a nice question, I am sorry. Are you praying all the time? That is a good thing, but God, he does not exist. No, he does not exist. (*Pause.*) I cannot sleep and I have been lying down and my husband goes out. Have you seen him? he is a blond man, big?

Owen   He was going that way (*He points.*), but . . .

Lotte   Many thanks! Many thanks! I must find him, I must find what he is doing . . .

She rushes off.

Owen   . . . but he didn't go that way, he went that way.

He points to where **Hannes** *actually did go.*

He puts his hands to his head again.

Owen   Nothing! Nothing! Nothing!

He starts to shake his head, the shaking gradually becoming more vigorous. **Hannes** *now appears carrying* **Evelyn** *over his shoulder. She is struggling with him.* **Hannes** *puts* **Evelyn** *down.* **Owen** *starts to calm down.*

Evelyn   Go on then, get it over with, ravish me!

Hannes   I cannot ravish you, I am a married man.

Evelyn   I don't care if you're married or not, just get on with it!

Hannes   You were trying to kill yourself in the sea.

Evelyn   When you're done ravishing me, you can just dump me back in it. At least I'll have had some pleasure before I went.

Hannes   Evelyn . . . why were you trying to kill yourself?

Evelyn   Oh, it's a long story.

Clara and **Ella** *appear. Slowly* **Evelyn** *starts to cry. This time her tears are real, less for effect than they normally are. This continues for some time as everyone watches her. As she recovers, she looks up and sees everyone looking at her.*

Evelyn   What are you all gawking at? What's wrong, have you all never seen a woman at the end of her tether before? Well, now the show's over. There's an idea, but, we could put on special shows. Tonight the madam of the establishment will try to drown herself. Extra helpings at breakfast for the hero who saves her. Wouldn't that be nice. What do you think, Attila? You're tonight's hero. An extra rasher for you in the morning.

Hannes   I think you should go home and be dry.

Evelyn   Always practical, you Huns. One day, one of you fellas says to me, and it bucketing down, there is no such thing as bad weather, only not being prepared for the weather you get. No such thing as bad weather! Did you ever hear the like! So, I'll stay here, wet and all as I am. I like the view. There's a great view from here, isn't there, Hannes?

Hannes   The fog is on the way.

Evelyn   Fog, well, how do you like that! Fog! (*Quietly.*) He offered me a lift home, and he said he had to pull over, visibility was hardly ten feet, and there in the car . . . (*She stops.*)

Clara *approaches her.*

Clara   You can tell us . . . it's time . . .

Evelyn   Since when is it time? Since when are you the one to tell me it's time?

Clara   It ruined your life and it's time . . .

Evelyn   Who says my life is ruined? Are you saying my life is ruined? The cheek of you! Are you my judge and jury? If anyone's going to say it, it's me. My life's ruined. It is. Was from a long time ago. I know that. I knew that. Everything since has just been getting on with it. There, that's it, sad, but true. Day by day, breakfast by breakfast, sausage by sausage. That's how I get through it, pull the frying pan out every morning, and then I just hope the doorbell rings. Yeh, well, it's something, isn't it? But I suppose next thing you're going to turn around and tell me all my troubles would be solved if I got myself a man, even for one night, if I were to jump the bones of Attila the Hun here to thank him for saving my life . . .

She has put her arms around **Hannes**.

You find me attractive, don't you, Hannes?

Hannes   Yes, I do, but . . .

Evelyn   You wouldn't throw me out of your bed? You wouldn't expect me to wear a bag over my head, would you?

Lotte *appears.*

Lotte   Hello . . . (*She stops.*) . . . Hannes . . . here you are . . . what is going on?

Hannes   She fell into the sea . . . and I was walking there . . . and I rescued her.

Lotte   And are you still rescuing her?

Hannes *puts* **Evelyn** *lying on the ground.*

Hannes   You will be OK now.

Evelyn   Yes, yes . . . thank you . . . for saving me . . . my hero!

Lotte   He is a very brave man.

Evelyn   And he's very strong. Very, very strong.

Lotte   I woke up, Hannes, and you were not there. There is no one there, but the girl who is having a baby.

Evelyn *springs up.*

Evelyn   She's having the baby?

Lotte   No, not having the baby now. She will have the baby. Hannes, come! We will go for a walk.

Evelyn   Jesus, you had me worried there, that B&B isn't due for a few weeks yet . . .

Hannes   Goodbye. You must go home and be dry.

Evelyn   Anything for my hero.

Lotte *leads* **Hannes** *away.* **Owen** *looks about and seems to get agitated and his hands get tense.*

Owen   Evelyn . . . Evelyn . . .

Ella   Mum . . . Did he rape you? (*Pause.*) Well, did he?

Evelyn   What do you want to know for?

Ella   Mum!

Evelyn   What?

Ella   Did he rape you?

Owen   Evelyn . . . Evelyn . . .

Owen's *hands get more tense.*

Evelyn   Owen, are you all right?

Ella   Mum, will you answer me! I've a right to know!

Evelyn   Who says?

Ella   I say.

Owen   When it was done . . . I just sat there, doing nothing . . . and all I could think of was the night you came home after your first kiss, Evelyn . . .

Evelyn   Owen, are you all right? What are you muttering about there?

Ella   Mum!

Evelyn   Yes, love?

Ella   Mum, you're going to answer me. He did rape you, didn't he?

Evelyn   I'm not answering any more questions. I nearly drowned just now, didn't I?

Owen   Evelyn . . . I sat there thinking of your first kiss . . . and then . . .

Ella *grabs her.*

Ella   Mum!

Evelyn   Yes, love?

Ella *shakes* **Evelyn**.

Ella   Mum!

Evelyn   Yes, love?

Ella   Mum!!

Evelyn   Yes, love?

Ella   Did he rape you? Did he? Did he?

Evelyn   I fancied him.

Ella *stops for a second, then shoves her away.*

Ella   What?

Evelyn   All the girls did. He was young enough, not old anyway . . . not bad-looking . . . no Paul Newman of course, but . . .

Ella (*barely able to speak*)   You fancied him . . . I can't believe this . . . this is just the worst thing ever . . . my God, my God, my God . . . I can't believe this . . . it's unfuckingbelievable . . .

The light from the lighthouse sweeps around. The sound of the foghorn.

No, no, no . . . there's only one thing for it now . . . you fancied him . . . a priest . . . oh my God . . . I'm going to have to drown myself now . . . it's the only thing for it . . .

She runs off. **Clara** *watches her go, then follows.* **Owen** *looks at his hands, shakes his head.*

Evelyn   What's she talking about, going to drown herself! I'm the one that says things like that! (*Looks at* **Owen**.) Well, it's just you and me left, Owen.

She approaches him.

Oh, Owen, where was my big brother all these years when I needed him.

She tries to embrace him. He shrinks away.

Owen   You . . . you . . . fancied him!

Evelyn   We all did . . . young girls . . . you know . . .

Owen   All . . . for . . . what then? All for . . . Evelyn . . . it was all a mistake . . . all a waste . . . my life . . .

Evelyn   Oh, for God's sake, Owen, will you give over. You lived the life you lived . . .

Owen   But, Evelyn, if it wasn't for him, think of the life I could've had here . . . I might've married, had kids of my own . . . I would've been able to come to your wedding . . . seen

Ella and Emer from the day they were born . . . think of all of that . . .

Evelyn   Yes, that's a lot . . . but you had good times.

Owen   What good times?

Evelyn   You tell me.

Owen   None.

Evelyn   Owen, don't say that.

Owen   None, Evelyn, and I didn't mind . . . until you said . . . you fancied him . . .

Evelyn   Look, Owen, I just said that in the heat of the moment.

Owen   The heat of the moment!

Evelyn   Owen, no life's wasted . . . except mine. Stuck in that B&B with two ungrateful daughters and a fornicating husband! There you were out in Las Vegas leading the high life!

Owen   Evelyn . . .

He looks at his hands and holds them in a choking gesture, then looks at **Evelyn***.*

The light sweeps around. **Ella** *comes back in, and collapses between* **Owen** *and* **Evelyn***.* **Clara** *follows.*

Ella   I tried to drown myself as well, Mum, but I couldn't do it. The water was fuckin' freezing.

Evelyn   I could've warned you about that . . . I had the same problem myself . . . and watch your language.

Evelyn *puts her arms around* **Ella***.* **Clara** *sees something.*

Clara   Emer! Emer!

Evelyn   Don't tell me she's going to try and drown herself as well.

Ella (*to herself*)   She would turn up!

Emer *comes in with the sack.*

Evelyn   What have you got there, love?

Emer   I've been having bad dreams about the skeleton baby again . . . ever since this . . . came into the house. I was going to throw it in the sea.

Ella   You were going to throw Dad away!

Evelyn   Maybe somebody would've got drowned tonight after all.

Emer *puts the sack down and sits down with* **Evelyn**, **Ella** *and* **Owen**.

Emer   Mum, what's everyone doing here?

Ella   Mum tried to drown herself.

Evelyn   So did Ella.

Emer   Oh.

Evelyn   Neither of us managed it.

Emer   Small mercies.

Ella   What's that supposed to mean?

Emer   Me to know, you to find out.

Evelyn   Now, no squabbling. Just for this minute, before your mother is moved upstairs to the grandmother division, and she doesn't matter any more with you having a baby, and you, Ella, yes, you, Ella . . . doing your thing . . .

She embraces both of them.

Yes, here we all are.

The light starts to sweep over them. It stops on **Clara** *as she speaks, making it look like a follow spot.*

Clara   And they'd all sit there for just that moment, not knowing what to do, what to say, as if they could stay there for ever, as if the lighthouse would flash past them for all time, protecting them, reassuring them, as if somehow, in the reach of its beam, everything was going to be just fine, and I felt outside them all, cut off from them, sitting where my father used to sit, looking out at the lighthouse, and afterwards I'd always remember the love I felt for Ella just then, even though I knew it would not last, even though I felt it slipping away as the beam swept past me . . .

The beam sweeps off **Clara** *and continues as a lighthouse beam. The sound of the foghorn.*

Emer Mum, I'm going to go to Gianni, when the baby's born.

Evelyn Yes, love, you could do that, you could . . .

Ella He won't want to know.

Emer We'll see.

Evelyn *turns to* **Owen**.

Evelyn Owen. (*Pause.*) Owen.

Owen Why did I kill him, Evelyn? Why?

Owen *shakes his head. The sound of the foghorn. The beam sweeps past once more.*

Act Five

Evelyn *sweeps the floor of the kitchen aggressively.*

Evelyn   Someday I'll escape this Bed and Burden of a place! Some day! (*Nods her head.*) Next time I will drown myself. Just have to make sure the sea is a bit warmer and there's no Hannes the Hun about to come to the rescue. Bed and Bedamned! Bed and Bollox! Bed and Bastard . . .

She puts the brush away and goes to the cooking area to start the breakfast. **Hannes** *appears in the door and watches her. He approaches slowly.* **Evelyn** *turns around with a tray in her hands and jumps when she sees him.*

Hannes   Evelyn.

Evelyn   Mr Kippenhan.

Hannes   Hannes.

Evelyn   Hannes.

Hannes   Or you can call me Johnnie. Hannes, it is short for Johannes, and Johannes is John in German, so you can call me Johnnie.

Evelyn   You're up early . . . Johnnie.

Hannes   What is it you say, the early bird he gets the worm.

Evelyn   You want worms for breakfast? Now, that'd be a first. I'll just go out back and turn over a few sods and pull out a few, and what do you do with them, throw them in to the frying pan or what?

Hannes *laughs.*

Hannes   You are very funny, Evelyn. I like your sense for humour. Is it not a thing you say in English, about the early bird?

Evelyn   We say a lot of things in English.

Hannes Evelyn . . . are you OK?

Evelyn Never been better.

Hannes I remember last night. I cannot forget it.

Evelyn Oh yes, you're to get an extra rasher this morning. How did I guess you wouldn't let me forget that?

Hannes It wasn't Lotte who did not sleep last night, it was I. I made up my mind, I will not go back to Germany, I will stay here and leave Lotte.

Hannes *has been backing* **Evelyn** *into a corner.*

Evelyn Oh, no, no, Herr Kippenhan, you wouldn't want that . . . (*Looks around.*) . . . Where's everybody when I need them . . . Look, Hannes . . .

Hannes You can call me Johnnie, Evelyn . . .

Evelyn Johnnie . . . I'm finished with men, gave them up same time I gave up chewing gum . . .

Owen *comes in the door.*

Evelyn Owen, you're up?

Owen *sits down at the table.*

Owen He doesn't let me sleep.

Evelyn You were looking for more toast, weren't you, Herr Kippenhan?

Hannes Johnnie.

Evelyn Johnnie.

She ushers **Hannes** *out the door.*

Owen Where is he?

Evelyn Who?

Owen You know who.

Evelyn   Oh, Father Molloy? I put him in the press with the pots and pans. D'ye know what I was thinking of doing, I thought I'd use the skull as a toiletbrush holder for the guests' toilet in the hall? I'd need to attach it to some kind of base so it wouldn't rock . . .

She rushes out with a tray of things. The door opens and **Emer** *struggles into the kitchen, groaning.*

Emer   Mum, Mum, my waters broke!

Evelyn *rushes back in.* **Emer** *groans.*

Emer   Mum, it's started!

Evelyn   What's started?

Emer *cries out and falls into* **Evelyn***'s arms.*

Evelyn   That's all I need in the middle of breakfast!

Emer   Mum, I don't want to give birth to a skeleton!

Emer *moans and groans throughout the following.*

Evelyn   No, you won't, it's going to be a healthy baby. (*Looks to* **Owen**.) Now, see what you've done, digging up skeletons from the past! The child'll be premature and if there's anything wrong with it, you're to blame!

Owen   Why did I kill him, Evelyn, why?

Evelyn   Owen, to be honest, at the moment, I don't give a Bed and Bedamned, haven't I a Bed and Bastard on the way in the middle of breakfast!

Owen   Evelyn, I've just wasted my life.

Evelyn   You could do something useful with your life now and call Dr Whelan! The number's over the phone.

Owen   Evelyn . . . I was thinking about Gayle all night.

Evelyn   You never mentioned her . . . Gayle?

Owen   She was expecting . . . the child would be fifteen now . . . and that was the end of it . . . she met some guy from Texas . . .

Evelyn   Ah, for the love of God, Owen, that's spilt milk from fifteen years ago, then!

Owen   Seems like yesterday.

Evelyn   Well, it's not. (**Emer** *screams.*) It's all right, love, your mother's here.

Emer   Mum, I don't want it to be a skeleton! Mum! Mum!

Owen (*stretching out his hands*)   I've wasted my life. (*Shouts.*) I've wasted my life.

Evelyn   No, you haven't! You've lived the life you've led, and that's all there's to it! Now, can you call Dr Whelan!

Ella *comes in and sits down.*

Evelyn   Ella, call Dr Whelan, and then get me some towels.

Ella *doesn't move.*

Evelyn   Ella!

Ella   What?

Evelyn   Your sister is going to have the baby now.

Ella   What, here?

Evelyn   Yes! Now, do what I told you! For once in your life!

Ella *goes to the phone.*

Evelyn   Lie down here, love.

She gets her on the ground.

It's all right, love, just you relax and breathe in deeply, like this.

She shows her how to breathe and we hear **Emer** *doing it.*

Lotte *appears at the door.* **Evelyn** *looks up.*

Evelyn   Toast is finished for the day.

Lotte   You are having a baby in the kitchen!

Evelyn   Go away, go away!

Lotte   I have done midwife courses in Germany. I can help.

She joins **Evelyn**. **Hannes** *appears at the door.*

Hannes, go away, or you will be sick, you know you will.

Hannes *continues to stare.*

Ella   Dr Whelan is out on a call. They've left a message on his mobile. (*About towels.*) Is that enough? Is it?

Evelyn   Yes, that'll do.

Lotte   Now we need a basin of water. (*To* **Emer**.) Now, that's good, breathe like this . . .

She tries to help **Emer** *with her breathing.* **Evelyn** *picks up the swatter and throws it at* **Owen**.

Evelyn   And Owen, if you want something else useful to do with your life, you keep an eye out for bluebottles! I don't want them dive-bombing in on this.

Lotte (*to* **Evelyn**)   It is lucky I am staying here.

Evelyn   I couldn't've planned it better.

Lotte   It is a very interesting place to stay, your Bed and Breakfast.

Evelyn   Make sure you tell all your friends about it.

Lotte   Hannes, he wants to come back all the time.

Evelyn   Does he? He must like the breakfast.

Owen *goes to the press and takes the sack out, then goes back to the table and sits down.* **Hannes** *begins to heave and he rushes to the sink, but manages to contain himself.* **Owen** *looks into the bag.*

Owen   She fancied you, she said . . . she fancied you! You! You!

Ella *brings a basin of water. The doorbell rings.*

Evelyn   Get that, Ella.

Ella   Now? We can't take guests in now, can we?

Evelyn   It might be Dr Whelan.

Ella *goes out.*

Evelyn   That's it, love, that's it.

Lotte   Push! Push! That's it!

Clara *appears above the set.* **Ella** *comes back in.*

Ella   A couple, looking for a room. What'll I do?

Evelyn   Send them away! No, don't! Tell them to come back later, or they'll end up in that fleapit of Tricia Burns's!

Ella *rushes out.* **Owen** *collapses to the floor. No one notices.*

Evelyn   Come on now, love, push the B&B out!

Emer   He's not a B&B! He's not! He's not, Mum!

Evelyn   All right, he's not then!

Ella *comes back in.*

Ella   Can I do anything else?

Evelyn   No, just stay out of the Bed and Bedamned way.

Ella *goes back to the table and she sees* **Owen** *on the ground. She kneels down to* **Owen**.

Ella   Uncle Owen! Uncle Owen!

She tries to turn him over. Just as she does, **Emer** *screams, and she jumps and falls against the sack.*

Evelyn   Come on, Emer, you can do it. Push! Push!

Clara *appears in the kitchen and she goes to* **Ella**. **Ella** *looks at* **Clara** *for a few moments, and the action stops.*

Clara   But I could tell from the way Ella looked at me that morning it was the end for us. The end of a lot of things that morning . . . and the beginning of others. Sometimes our lives seem to form themselves into chapters, and while we are living through it, we cannot see how things are forming, it's only afterwards that we can put a shape on it . . .

Then **Clara** *and* **Ella** *nod to each other, the action re-commences and* **Clara** *and* **Ella** *start to disassemble the set, pushing away the walls etc. In the background the lighthouse, the blue sea. Music plays faintly and will come in and out through most of the rest of the act.*

Emer's *screams get louder.* **Hannes** *vomits in the sink as the wall is moved.*

Emer   I can't! I can't! I'm going to die! Gianni! Gianni! Where are you, you fucker! You fucker! Mum! Mum! I'm going to die! I know I am, I know I am!

Evelyn   No, you're not! Push, come on, push! (**Emer** *groans.*) That's it, love, that's it! There's the head! There's the head! You're nearly there. Push, now! Push! The last time!

Lotte   Push! Push! Push!

Emer   Come out, you Bed and Bastard! Come out! You Bed and Bastard! You Bed and Bastard! (*She repeats this a number of times, shouting more and more.*)

She screams and the baby is born. **Evelyn** *and* **Lotte** *wrap the baby up, and give it to* **Emer**.

Emer   Is he OK? Is he OK?

Lotte   He is a healthy boy!

Emer   Great . . . great . . .

She fades away. **Evelyn** *gets a basket and they place the baby in it.* **Clara** *and* **Ella** *move the kitchen table and chairs away from the centre of the space.*

Clara   Now, when I think about it, it is hard to imagine so much happening under one roof that day.

Ella   That was a day.

Clara *goes to her and they embrace, then separate, and then look at each other.*

Evelyn *takes a chair and sits down, burying her face in her hands.*

Emer   Mum, Mum, I want to phone Dad.

Evelyn   Who?

Emer   Dad.

Evelyn   For what?

Emer   To tell him . . . I want to be able to tell somebody . . .

Evelyn *goes to the phone, and as she is dialling, she sees* **Owen** *on the ground.*

Evelyn   Owen, Owen . . . (*Listens.*) . . . hello? Eddie, no, no, I was talking to Owen. He's home, and he's dug him up and your daughter just had her baby . . . (*Listens.*) . . . yes, had her baby, and now Owen's dead. (*Listens.*) No, Eddie, keep your hair on! The baby's not dead, Owen is, the baby's fine, just couldn't wait to drop in on this mess of a world . . .

She hands the phone to **Emer**.

Evelyn   Your father . . .

Emer   Dad, Dad, he's a lovely boy . . .

Evelyn *goes back to* **Owen**. **Ella** *approaches.*

Evelyn   Owen. (*She touches him.*) One in, one out, puts a brake on the increase in the world's population, eh? Owen . . . Owen . . . Owen . . .

She starts to cry. To one side, **Hannes** *and* **Lotte** *have their suitcases.*

Ella   You OK, Mum?

Evelyn   It's all come asunder . . . I spent years trying to hold it all together, now it's come down about my ears. After . . . all I wanted was a normal life . . . a normal life . . . We were the perfect family, we really were, Eddie was going well with his accountancy . . . but it slipped out, one night . . . it was Christmas, we'd been talking about Owen, I always missed him at Christmas. It was only a little thing, and the drink didn't help . . . only a little thing I said . . . about Owen giving up everything for me . . . and Eddie, he's very smart, he asked question after question, wanted to get to the bottom of it, and he got it out of me . . . and see where letting the cat out of the bag got me . . .

She looks down at **Owen**.

I used to miss him at Christmas all right. We were very close, when our parents weren't getting on . . . (*She shakes her head.*) . . . I didn't know about Gayle . . . about the child that never was . . . he didn't have much of a life it seems . . . oh, Owen, Owen. . .

Ella   Are you sure he's dead, Mum?

Evelyn *begins to cry.* **Ella** *touches him.* **Owen** *begins to stir, and* **Ella** *jumps back.* **Owen** *sits up and looks around, dazed.*

Evelyn   And now it's Lazarus.

Owen   Oh . . . I thought I was . . . somewhere else . . .

Evelyn   And me wasting my tears over you!

Owen *gets to his feet, staggering a little.*

Owen   Evelyn, do you remember the time you got stung by a bee? You were in our garden and you were sitting on an orange crate, and you made a crown for yourself, so you were the queen. And a bee landed on one of the flowers and you ordered it to go away, and of course, it wouldn't, so you tried to hit it with the sceptre you'd made yourself, and, well, the bee didn't like it very much, being hit, so it stung you on the arm. You came running in to me, and I did my best to deal with the sting: I sucked at your arm and put ointment on it.

Evelyn   Yeh? What about it?

Owen   I just remembered it.

Evelyn   Is there a point to that?

Owen   No. (*Pause.*) I just remembered it. I've forgotten a lot of things like that . . . things that mean nothing . . . things that have nothing to do with . . . just an innocent little thing I remembered . . .

Evelyn   Just remembering things is a waste of time, if you ask me.

Owen   Little things like that coming at me in my head all the time now . . . (*He smiles.*)

Owen *looks about.* **Ella** *approaches* **Evelyn**.

Ella   Mum, I always knew there was something up. I could tell. The different way you looked at Emer.

Evelyn   No, I didn't, love.

Ella (*emphatically*)   Yes, you did!

Evelyn   She was just the younger child . . . it's not unusual . . . you know . . . the older always gets jealous . . .

Ella   I wasn't jealous of her. Never was, never will be. (*Laughs.*) Just look at her . . . (*Then she turns to* **Clara**, *then turns to the audience.*) And I poured scorn over my younger sister. But doing it I knew I was fooling myself because, in truth, I knew my scorn would not hold up. That she turned out more beautiful than me was something I could tell every day from the looks of the male guests, and that only fed the rivalry between us, and if she thought I was interested in one, she would do her best to get in ahead of me. That's what happened with Gianni.

Hannes *and* **Lotte** *come up to* **Evelyn**.

Hannes   This is the best moment of my life.

Evelyn   Is it?

Hannes   Me and Lotte, we're going to move to Ireland. We want to die here.

Evelyn   Do you?

Hannes   Yes, don't we, Lotte?

Lotte   Yes, right here.

Evelyn   Well, if you need a room to do your dying in, just come right back here!

Lotte   We are going now.

Evelyn   Thank you very much.

Lotte   She is asleep now, and the baby as well. Soon you must get her into a bed. And the doctor to see the baby.

Hannes   We will come again.

Evelyn   Tell all your friends. Never a dull moment, eh? It's always like this.

Hannes   No, I know it is not, it is just your sense for humour, I know.

Lotte *signals for* **Hannes** *to go.*

Hannes   Goodbye. (*He goes.*)

Lotte   I cannot sleep at night because for a lot of years since I have been wanting to leave Hannes. I think about it every night when he is in the bed beside me. Now, I have changed my mind. I will not leave him. Goodbye.

Lotte *walks away and joins* **Hannes**, *who looks back at* **Evelyn** *and waves.*

Ella   Mum, do you remember once you told me something? Dad was after banishing me to my room for telling lies, I'd taken some money you left on the kitchen table, and I made up that I saw someone running away from the house.

Evelyn (*thinking*)   No . . . no . . . I don't remember, love.

Ella   Well, you came up to my room to tell me I was wrong to steal, but that sometimes you have to tell lies. (*Pause.*) You were right.

Evelyn   I said that? (*Pause.*) I shouldn't've said that, that wasn't something to say to a child.

Ella   We can bury him again, and say nothing.

Owen *grabs the sack.*

Owen   No, no, no . . . we have to . . . I have to . . .

Ella   You'll be dead, it won't matter to you.

Evelyn   Ella, don't talk like that to your uncle.

Ella   But, Mum, it's you and me that'll . . . (*She stops.*) Mum, what do you want?

Evelyn   Me? Want? To head off to Timbuktu and never come back!

Ella   Mum!

Evelyn   What, love?

Ella   Mum! What do you want to do?

Evelyn (*listens*)   Where's that doorbell when I need it?

Ella   Mum!

Evelyn   I love that doorbell, really. I give out all the time, I know, but if that doorbell wasn't going to ring, I don't know how I'd get out of bed in the morning, even if some of them would drive you mad. (*Pause.*) Ring, doorbell, ring, till I'm Bed and Bedead!

Ella Mum!

The music becomes more dominant.

Clara I'd split up with Ella soon enough. It was as if the events of those days were too much for her, too much for us. She'd say it'd've been better if she never knew, but the choice wasn't hers. Once the story was out in the open, there was no forgetting it, no avoiding it, and she'd wear it like a pair of dark glasses. She helped Evelyn for a while with the B&B, until she fell in love with a guest. He was English, from Bristol, and she ended up living over there for a couple of years, but it wouldn't last . . .

Ella *turns to* **Clara***, takes her hand, and kisses her on the cheek.*
Emer *wakes up and looks around.*

Emer Hi, Mum.

Evelyn *rushes to her.*

Evelyn How are you, love?

Emer (*alarmed*) Where is he? Where is he?

Evelyn Here.

She gives her the baby.

A grandmother and I'm not even forty! Ella, don't let me forget about those condom machines . . .

She shakes her head and looks over at **Emer***, and can't help smiling.*

Emer I'm going to call him Giovanni, Mum.

Evelyn (*shocked*) You can't!

Emer Why not?

Evelyn Well, it's your choice, but . . . Giovanni . . . another Don Giovanni . . . (*She laughs.*)

Emer He's beautiful, isn't he, Mum?

Evelyn Of course he is . . . a beautiful Bed and Bas – . . .

Emer   Mum!

Evelyn   Yeh, I know, love, yes, he is beautiful . . .

She takes the sack off **Owen**.

And I have you to thank for that, you . . .

She strikes at the sack and kicks at it a few times, but stops and shakes her head.

Someday I'll forgive you, I want to, I'm trying to . . . now
. . . but . . . but . . . it beats me . . .

She shakes her head and puts the sack down, then goes to the fridge and looks into it.

Ella, remind me to ring the butcher and order in more
sausages, I'm nearly out.

Ella   Yes, Mum.

Evelyn   Ella . . .

Ella   Yeh, Mum?

Evelyn   You're mine, a hundred per cent mine. (*Pause.*)
Ella?

Ella   I hear you, Mum.

Evelyn   And I better get in more cornflakes. (*Listens.*) No,
the bluebottles are on a day off, at least that's something.

Emer *turns to the audience as* **Evelyn** *looks in the cupboards.*

Emer   I would go to Italy to look for Gianni. But when I
found his house, I'd be told he'd gone off to Germany to
work and they didn't know where he was. They were
supposed to send his address in Germany when they got it.
The address never arrived. I knew it wouldn't, I was just
happy to have met his parents, for my child to have met his
other grandparents.

The baby wakes up crying. **Emer** *stills it.*

Evelyn   I'll be off down to the police station with that sack soon enough. I knew Owen needed that before . . . (*She stops.*) They'll be all over us then, TV people, journalists, photographers. And we'll be the most unpopular family in the parish, because we'll have dragged everyone else into it. I wasn't the only one interfered with. There were others. They'll have to remember then.

Owen *puts the bag over his shoulder.*

Owen   He'll get a quiet funeral, a small gathering of family and clergy, and it'll be reported on the television and I'll feel happy seeing him buried. There'll be those who'll come up to me and say quietly I did right all those years ago killing him, but that I should've left him where he was . . . and others who'd look away if they saw me out walking, and others who'd just bless themselves . . .

Evelyn *has the swatter in her hand, and she swats vigorously.*

Evelyn   No, no, I'm imagining bluebottles now.

Owen   Evelyn, we've something to do.

Evelyn   Yes, of course, of course we have. But there's always time for tea. We can have a cup of tea first, can't we?

Owen   We can. Evelyn?

Evelyn   Yes?

Owen   I remember the night I waited for you to come home from your date with Eddie Dwyer . . . and you'd asked me that day if you should kiss him . . . and that evening you came home and smiled at me . . . your first kiss.

Evelyn   Did I really ask you that? I don't remember. I do remember him kissing me for the first time. Eddie . . . he was a good kisser . . .

Clara *moves to the background where the panorama of the sea and the lighthouse is.*

Evelyn (*to* **Emer**)   Is your father coming to see the child?

Emer   He said he'd be here tomorrow.

Evelyn   That's good. He'll be happy. He was good with you girls, he was . . . (*Listens.*) . . . that doorbell's been very quiet. Where's the Bed and Bedlam? That Patricia Burns must be out stealing them all for her fleapit, she's a bit cheaper but are her rooms en suite? They are not!

She looks to **Clara**, *as does everyone else.*

Clara   And after, in the pubs, on the street corners, in the shops, the story would do the rounds, of how Owen Mahon came home from Las Vegas with a tumour on his brain, so as to make his peace. Owen would be charged and released on bail and he'd die under Evelyn's roof six months later before a case could be brought. It was one of the biggest funerals seen in these parts, and even the Bishop came, and that was seen as significant, as some form of reconciliation. But Evelyn would never say what happened, she would always avoid answering that one. Maybe she was protecting him, maybe she was protecting herself or Ella, or maybe she just wanted the real heart of the secret to be hers, and hers only, and I am sure she would wrestle with that one, fight with herself ever afterwards.

Evelyn   It beats me . . . (*Shakes her head.*) . . . yeh, it beats me . . .

Clara   And after the reports in the papers, on the radio, on the television faded away, all that was left was the story, and it would excite the tongues for many months, many years, before going cold, but it would be part of the fabric of the place and as I lead people around, ladies and gentlemen, I point to the house and then out to the lighthouse and tell a brief version of this story, and who knows but that in a hundred years time people will still point to the same landmarks and tell the same story . . .

They all look at each other, towards the audience, as the music rises to a crescendo.

Printed in the USA
CPSIA information can be obtained
at www.ICGtesting.com
LVHW041101171024
794057LV00001B/190